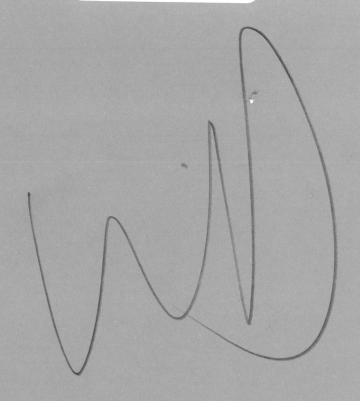

THE COOK'S GUIDE TO FISH & SEAFOOD

THE COOK'S GUIDE TO FISH & SEAFOOD

Wendy Sweetser

Illustrated by Jane Laurie

APPLE

A Quintet Book

First published in the UK in 2009 by
Apple Press
7 Greenland Street
London NW1 0ND
United Kingdom

www.apple-press.com

ISBN: 978-1-84543-333-8
QTT.GGF

This book was conceived, designed and produced by
Quintet Publishing Limited
The Old Brewery, 6 Blundell Street
London N7 9BH, UK

Project Editor: Robert Davies
Designer: Emma Wicks
Copy Editor: Nicole Foster
Art Director: Michael Charles
Managing Editor: Donna Gregory
Publisher: James Tavendale

10 9 8 7 6 5 4 3 2 1

Printed in China by 1010 Printing International Limited

CONTENTS

Introduction

As well as being delicious, fish are easy to prepare, quick to cook, infinitely versatile and healthy too, which makes them an essential component of a modern diet.

No modern culinary fad, fish were the first animals with a backbone (vertebrates) to appear on earth over 500 million years ago and, in the intervening millennia, all kinds of creatures have developed from those first primitive fish to swim the world's oceans, rivers and lakes and feed its people.

Some fish, like cod, snapper, bream and gurnard, belong to huge families with many species found in far-flung corners of the globe, often with different names. Some like John Dory and flying fish are unique, while others – the Japanese fugu springs to mind – not only look scary, but have the potential to condemn any fish-lover who chooses to eat it to a swift and painful death.

We think of fish as cold-blooded, water-dwelling creatures with gills, fins, backbones, scales and streamlined bodies but, as with most things in nature, not all fish conform to that stereotype. It's true they all live in water and breathe through gills but eels don't have fins, lampreys have no bones, catfish, cod and mackerel are just some of the fish with no scales, and monkfish, with its giant head and ferocious teeth, is not many people's idea of a sleek, streamlined beauty.

Among the flotilla of other watery creatures living alongside fish we find crabs and lobsters with long claws and tough carapaces that scuttle along the seabed rather than swim. There are molluscs that cling to rocks, corals or special ropes dropped for them into the sea, the cephalopod family of cuttlefish, squid and octopus with their soft, rubbery bodies and 8 or 10 arms and legs, sea urchins armed to defend themselves with coats of many spikes, and many, many more.

The wealth of fish living all around us is endless and varied and we should do all we can to respect and protect this rich source of food. Fish and seafood are a treat to be enjoyed, and hopefully this book will inspire you to experiment with new varieties that perhaps you haven't tried before, to seek out local species on your travels and persuade your family and friends that fish really is good for them!

From sea, river or lake to table

The public's desire for fish saw its first surge in the Middle Ages in Europe, when churches decreed that good Christians shouldn't eat meat on Fridays, during Lent or on other fast days.

For the faithful who lived by the sea, eating fish on Fridays wasn't a problem, but for those living inland, supply couldn't match demand, so estates, castles and monasteries turned to their local ponds, streams and rivers with their abundant stocks of freshwater pike, bream and trout.

Fish is highly perishable so, in the days before widespread refrigeration, other ways of conserving catches had to be found. Preserving techniques such as drying and salting were first developed by the Greeks and Romans and later adopted elsewhere. Merchants and traders found they could have a good supply of fish to sustain them on long journeys, and other maritime communities preserved large seasonal catches such as cod that lasted all year.

For fresh fish to arrive at our tables and be at its best it must be packed in ice and kept cold from the moment it is caught until it reaches market. Much of the fish we buy today is frozen which, as long as this is done on-board ship as soon as it is caught, is no bad thing, because it ensures the fish remains in peak condition for an extended period. Freezing under less controlled conditions, carried out at fluctuating temperatures and not immediately after catching, can cause ice crystals to form in the flesh of the fish, to the detriment of its texture and flavour.

How fish are caught

Many different methods are used to catch fish, from the deep-sea trawler to the boy with his homemade fishing line.

Diver-caught

Divers gather shellfish such as scallops and clams by hand, selecting only the biggest and best.

Dredging

Used mainly for shellfish, dredging involves a large, heavy metal rake being dragged across the seabed. The downside of dredging is that it disturbs the habitats of other ocean life and can sweep up unwanted fish and sponges as bycatch. It can also fill the shells of molluscs such as scallops with grit and sand.

Fish farming

Also known by its more scientific name of aquaculture, fish and shellfish are farmed in a controlled environment. Salmon and tuna are typically raised in offshore open net pens or cages; other species will be raised in ponds and lakes, such as shrimp in mangrove forests. As fish grow to commercial size, they are harvested, processed as necessary and dispatched to market within hours.

Farmed fish might not conjure up the same romantic image as a fish caught in the wild, but properly husbanded farmed fish have distinct advantages:
• Supplies are regular rather than seasonal.
• They are cheaper, with more stable prices.
• Strict controls govern their production methods and catch size.
• They are often fresher than wild fish.
• They may have been raised in a better environment. For example, freshwater fish farmed in clean water will have a better flavour than similar fish caught in brackish or muddy streams in the wild.

Oysters, mussels and clams are farmed on beaches or offshore on ropes suspended in the sea and, as with filter feeders, their presence helps to keep the water they live in clean.

Currently around one-third of the world's seafood is farmed, with this figure bound to rise as the global demand for fish continues to increase. Salmon and prawns are both farm-raised and fished in the wild; other popular species such as catfish, tilapia and mussels are almost exclusively farmed.

Gillnetting

This involves a curtain of netting that hangs across a large stretch of water. Fish swim into the net and get trapped in the mesh. The size of mesh varies according to the species of fish being caught; larger mesh used to catch cod or salmon will allow smaller fish to pass through.

Harpooning

This is the traditional way to catch large fish such as bluefin tuna and swordfish and is still used today. A skilled fisherman is needed to identify his chosen catch, spear it with his harpoon, and haul it aboard his boat.

Hook and lining

Fishing rods or lines with one or more hooks are baited and then jerked in the water to simulate the motion of small fish, thus attracting larger fish to the bait. Once hooked, the catch is landed either manually or with a mechanised reel. Used to catch a variety of fish, from ocean-going tuna and mahi mahi to bottom dwellers such as cod.

Longlining

Fish are lured to a central fishing line that can stretch from 1 kilometre to more than 80 kilometres and is strung with smaller lines with baited hooks. Used at different depths to catch different fish – near the surface or just off the seabed – longlines that are close to the surface have the disadvantage of accidentally killing seabirds, turtles or sharks.

Pot trapping

A cage lowered onto the seabed with a buoy attached that floats on the surface to mark its position. Used for catching lobsters, crabs and sometimes bottom-dwelling fish such as sablefish. Once lured into the pot, the creature is held there alive until the pot is hauled up.

Purse seining

A purse seine is a large net used to encircle fish that swim in shoals, such as sardines and tuna. As the fish enter the net, the fishermen pull the bottom of it closed, like a drawstring bag, and the trapped fish are hauled into the boat still in the net or scooped out with smaller nets. Net design has recently been modified so that dolphins can be released.

Trawling

Boats tow cone-shaped nets behind them that drag along the seabed, stirring up shrimp, cod and flat fish and sweeping them into the net. Other trawlers set their nets mid-water to catch shoaling fish such as sardines. Trawl nets can accidentally trap endangered turtles and other fish and damage the seabed and habitat of other marine creatures. Nets have now been modified to allow bycatch to escape.

Trolling

This involves a boat towing baited lines behind or alongside it at different levels to catch fish such as salmon, albacore tuna and mahi mahi which are lured by a moving bait.

Sustainability

Reckless over-fishing during the last few decades has led to dangerously depleted stocks of many species of fish.

Environmentalists are fighting back with conservation programmes that include limiting the size of catches and how often boats can go out. There has been an increase in the number of responsibly managed fish farms, and more and more chefs are encouraging us, the customers, to experiment with lesser-known varieties not on the danger list.

The Marine Stewardship Council (MSC) was set up ten years ago in London as an independent, non-profit-making charity and now has offices around the world. Committed to promoting well-managed fishing practices, any fish or seafood – such as New Zealand hoki, Cornish mackerel and Alaska salmon – bearing the MSC's blue seal of approval logo is an indication to consumers that the fish is from a sustainable source.

In 1999, the Monterey Bay Aquarium in California also developed a list of sustainable seafood as part of their 1997–1999 'Fishing Solutions' exhibit. This list evolved into the 'Seafood Watch' pocket guide for consumers, which raises awareness about the importance of buying seafood from sustainable sources.

Why fish is good for you

Fish is one of the healthiest foods there is. White fish and most freshwater fish, with the exception of salmon, eels and trout, are a major source of proteins, minerals and vitamin B, and as they have virtually no fat they're great for weight-watchers too.

Oil-rich fish provide more energy than white fish, thanks to their higher levels of fat. They are packed with vitamin D, without which the body cannot absorb calcium, and they contain important levels of omega-3 polyunsaturated fatty acids. Although these fatty acids are essential for keeping us healthy, our bodies cannot manufacture them and we have to obtain them from the food we eat. Oil-rich fish is one of the most satisfying ways of doing this.

Omega-3's reputation for helping to prevent heart disease, improve brainpower and boost our immune system is well documented but recent research also suggests it can relieve the symptoms of arthritis and some skin problems as well.

The downside is that oily fish can contain higher levels of contaminants such as mercury than white fish. Health officials therefore recommend that adults eat no more than four portions of oily fish per week, while children, pregnant women and nursing mothers should limit their intake to two portions per week.

Shellfish contain similar nutrients to white fish, although levels of omega-3 vary. Crab and mussels are good sources of omega-3 but shrimp contain hardly any.

Ciguatera poisoning

Certain coral reef fish, such as those found in the Caribbean and the Pacific, feed on a group of marine planktons called dinoflagellates that are toxic if eaten. Although the recorded incidences of ciguatera poisoning are very low, it can result in skin rashes, severe headaches, weakness, vomiting and other unpleasant symptoms.

Large reef fish live on smaller, plankton-eating species and as the toxin remains in the food chain, the larger the fish the more toxic it becomes. Surgeonfish, barracuda, moray eels and some of the snapper family are particularly susceptible and as the toxins settle in the liver, this part of a reef fish should never be eaten.

Choosing fish and shellfish

When choosing fish and shellfish, be guided by three senses –
how they look, how they feel and how they smell.

• Fresh whole fish should have bright, clear, bulging eyes, shiny skin that feels firm when gently pressed and a clean smell. The gills should be red, rather than muddy brown, and if the fish has been gutted, the body cavity should be clean.

• Fresh bivalve molluscs such as mussels, scallops and clams should be tightly closed or close up when tapped. Discard any that have cracked shells or that do not open fully when cooked. Oysters must be bought alive because they deteriorate quickly and can cause serious food poisoning.

• Live crustaceans such as crabs and lobsters should react when touched and the tails of live lobsters, langoustines and crayfish should fold under the body.

• Cephalopods should have translucent white body flesh, smell fresh and have no red tinge to their outer membrane.

• Smoked fish such as mackerel or herring should be glossy with an oily sheen, and smell smoky and fresh.

• Frozen fish should be undamaged by freezer burn and prawns shouldn't have too thick an overcoat of ice.

Buying

As small, local fish merchants become an endangered species themselves, most of us are buying our fish from supermarkets.

Many larger supermarkets have well-stocked fish counters and trained staff on hand who are happy to prepare fish for you in the way you want. Those living by the sea can often buy from local fishermen or markets but markets located far inland are rarely the place to find the best fish and seafood as the produce may have travelled a long way, not necessarily under ideal conditions.

Approximately 50 per cent of the weight of a whole fish is edible flesh, although this will vary according to the species and cut required. As a rough guide, if serving whole fish allow 340–400g (12–14oz) per person. For fillets or steaks allow115–200g (4–7oz) per person, depending on the type of fish. White fish can be served in larger portions; oily fish such as salmon are richer so portions need to be smaller.

Storing

When you get a whole fresh fish home, store it on a plate or tray in the refrigerator covered with plastic wrap. The body cavity should be clean and the fish, apart from having its natural slime, should feel moist but should not be sitting in a pool of water.

Fillets and steaks should be stored in the same way as whole fish. Fish you've caught yourself will keep for around a week but fish bought from commercial outlets should be cooked and eaten within two to three days of purchase.

Molluscs and live crustaceans need to be covered with a damp cloth or seaweed in a covered container to prevent dehydration. Always pick up live crustaceans carefully by the body, never the claws or tail, or they could give you a painful nip. Oysters should be stored with their cupped shell downwards to retain their moisture. Shellfish should be eaten on the day of purchase or within 24 hours.

Keep smoked fish separate from raw fish in the refrigerator. Hot-smoked fish has a shorter shelf life than cold smoked.

Only freeze fish or shellfish that hasn't previously been frozen, although if cooked fish was frozen in its raw state it can be frozen again after cooking. To freeze, scale and gut if necessary and wrap the fish tightly in plastic wrap, followed by sealed foil to avoid its flesh being damaged by freezer burn. White fish can be frozen for four to six months, oily fish and shellfish for two to three months. Defrost frozen fish overnight in the refrigerator or cook from frozen.

Equipment

***No special equipment is needed to prepare fish but the
following will make the task quicker and easier.***

Fish scaler

This is a special metal tool with a long handle used
for removing the scales from fish. The top half –
usually shaped like a long thin fish – is covered with
small, round blunt blades which, when run down the
sides of a fish from tail to head, remove the scales
without damaging the skin. Although a scaler does
the job effectively, fish scales can be removed using
the back of a knife or the bowl of a shallow spoon.

Filleting knife

While any sharp kitchen knife with a pointed blade
will suffice, a proper filleting knife with a long,
flexible blade will make filleting easier.

Strong kitchen scissors or shears

A pair of heavy-duty kitchen scissors is useful for
snipping off fins and cutting through bones.

Tweezers

Pin boning becomes a whole lot easier when done
with tweezers or a small pair of pliers.

Large cutting board

If you prepare a lot of fish, it's worth keeping a board
especially for the task. After use, scrub the board
thoroughly in hot water with detergent and never
prepare raw and cooked fish on the board at the
same time.

Chopping knife

A heavy-bladed kitchen knife with a pointed
blade is needed for cutting off fish heads and other
general preparation.

Oyster knife

A stubby knife with a fat handle and thick, pointed
blade used for opening oysters.

Crab or lobster crackers

Looking like strong nutcrackers, these are used
for cracking the thick-shelled claws of crabs and
lobsters. A hammer or weight could be used instead,
but avoid bashing too hard and shattering the shell
into tiny fragments that lodge in the meat.

Trimming, scaling and gutting

*If you buy an ungutted fish or you catch your own, it is
important to 'clean' it as soon as possible or its insides will
begin to taint the flesh around the stomach. Before you do this,
first scale the fish, as the scales are easier to remove when
the fish is fresh and moist, and once the skin starts to dry
out, they will stick to it like glue!*

Round fish

Trimming
Soft fins can be left on, but with species like bass that have spiky fins it is important to snip these off with kitchen scissors

Scaling
Scales have a nasty habit of flying all over the place, so cover the work surface with newspaper before you start so you can wrap them up and throw the parcel away afterwards. Alternatively, do the job by holding the fish in a large plastic bag. It's not a good idea to scale a fish in the sink as you'll end up either blocking it up or picking the sticky pieces out of the plughole for days.

Hold the fish by its tail – if it's very slippery, wear a rubber glove or dip your fingers in salt – and scrape off the scales using a special scaling tool, or by running the back of a thick-bladed knife or the bowl of a spoon at a right angles to the fish, down each side from tail to head.

Cleaning
Lay the scaled fish on a board and, with a sharp knife or kitchen scissors, cut the belly open from where the anal fin was attached (the one nearest the tail on the underside) to the head. Scrape the guts out of the body cavity with a knife or your hands, using scissors to cut away any entrails that remain attached. Rinse the fish thoroughly inside and out under cold running water. If cleaning salmon or sea trout, look inside the cavity and scrape out any clotted blood on either side of the backbone with a pointed knife.

Flat fish

Trimming
Snip off the side fins using kitchen scissors.

Scaling
As few flat fish have scales this is usually unnecessary. Dover sole and brill are the exceptions and should be scaled in the same way as round fish.

Cleaning
To locate the gut cavity, press the white side of the skin below the head where there will be an area that feels softer than on the other side. Make an incision here and pull out the guts with your finger or a small knife. The roe can be left in and cooked with the fish, but if you prefer to remove it make a larger incision along the same side and lift the roe out.

Filleting

Filleting can be a tricky task for the uninitiated, so if you don't feel confident, ask for a whole fish to be filleted when you buy it, but keep any gelatinous bones as they make excellent stock. If, however, you do have to tackle filleting a fish yourself – either by choice or necessity – the following instructions should help.

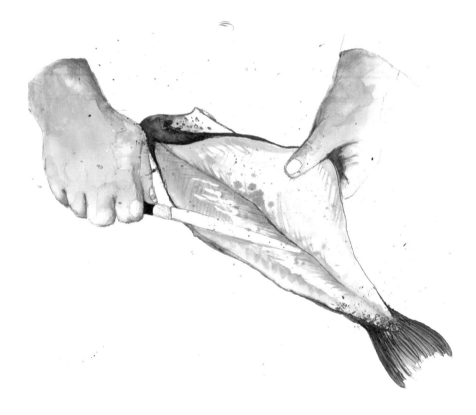

Round fish

Small fish, such as mackerel, herring and trout
Place the fish on a board with its back towards you
and cut across it from the underside diagonally
behind the head and through the backbone to cut
ff the head.

With the knife pointing towards the tail, cut into the
flesh at the head end and all the way down on one
side of the backbone to the tail, keeping the blade
of the knife flat against the bone as a guide. Lift off
the fillet in one piece and then turn the fish over and
repeat on the other side.

Alternative method for small fish
Cut off the head and all the way down the belly so
the fish can be opened out. Lay it on a board, skin
side up and press firmly along the backbone with
your thumbs to loosen the flesh from the bone. Turn
the fish over and carefully pull out the back and rib
bones all in one go, loosening any stubborn bones
with your fingers or the tip of a knife to avoid tearing
the flesh, and snipping the bone off with scissors
just above the tail. Remove any small bones left in
the flesh with your fingers, tweezers or a small pair
of pliers.

The flesh can be cut in half as two fillets or left as a
double 'butterfly' fillet. Double fillets can be cooked
as they are or filled with a stuffing, reshaped and
tied up with thin string before baking.

Larger fish
Lay the fish on a board and cut off the head behind
the gills, following the line of the gills in a V-shape
so as not to lose any of the fillet. Position the fish so
its back is towards you, and cut down the length of
the backbone and around the ribs in the same way
as for a smaller fish but lifting over the flap of fillet
as you proceed to make it easier to see where you
are going. Lift off the top fillet, turn the fish over and
repeat on the other side.

Filleting large round fish is a case of practice makes
perfect as it's easy to stray from the backbone
and cut into the fillet. The rib bones can also be
particularly tricky to remove. If you find it hard to
cut around them, such as with a salmon, cut through
the ribs and remove them afterwards by turning the
fillet over and pulling the bones out.

As well as filleting, large round fish can also be cut
across into steaks.

Pin boning
Pin bones are the tiny – but sharp and annoying –
bones that radiate out from the backbone and remain
in the flesh of some round fish, particularly salmon,
after the fillets have been taken off. To remove these,
lay the fillet skin side down on a board and feel
along the thickest part of the flesh with your fingers
to locate the row of pin bones running down its
length. Pull them out with tweezers, taking care not
to tear the flesh as you do so.

Flat fish

Flat fish are much easier to fillet than round fish due to their bone structure. Lay the fish on a board and make an incision down the backbone from head to tail. Starting at the head end, work the blade of the knife along one side of the cut towards the side edge of the fish, keeping the blade almost flat, until you can remove the fillet. Repeat with the remaining three fillets.

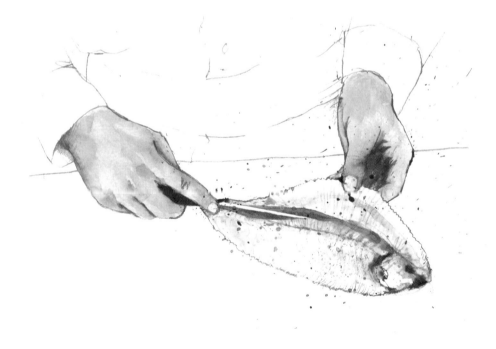

Skinning

Skinning a fish is often a matter of personal choice and generally the skin on the white side of a flat fish is eaten. Only when skin is very tough or could impart a bitter taste to the flesh is it necessary to remove it; otherwise it can be left on or removed as preferred.

Round fish and flat fish are skinned in the same way, the one exception being Dover sole.

Lay the fillet, skin side down, on a board, and hold the tail end with one hand. With the other, cut away from you, using a sawing motion up the flesh towards the head end, keeping the blade of the filleting knife quite flat and against the skin, until the flesh can be lifted away from the skin in one piece.

Skinning a Dover sole
Lay the whole fish dark side up on a board and cut across the skin just above the tail. Work your finger under the cut edge so the skin is loosened on each side just far enough for you to grip it. Sprinkle the tail end with salt to make it less slippery and grasp with one hand. Hold the loose skin and pull it sharply upwards right over the head of the fish. The skin on the white side can be left on or removed in the same way.

Preparing shellfish, crustaceans, molluscs and cephalopods

Prawns

Raw prawns can be cooked with their heads, tails and shells left on or they can be peeled first. Larger prawns need to be deveined to remove the dark thread running down their back. This thread is the prawn's feeding tube and, though safe to eat, can be gritty. To do this, cut down the centre back of the prawn, without cutting all the way through the flesh, with a sharp knife and pull out the thread with your fingers or the tip of the knife. To peel, cut off the head and tail of the prawn and strip off the shell with your fingers.

Crabs, lobsters and crayfish

Crabs, lobsters and crayfish are best cooked live because their flesh deteriorates rapidly after death. There are different ways of doing this but the most humane are given here.

To cook a live crab
First freeze it for two hours so it becomes unconscious. Prepare a strong brine – about 2 tablespoons salt to 950ml (32 fl oz) water – and heat this gently in a large pan, stirring until the salt dissolves. Bring to a rolling boil, add the frozen crab and simmer for 15 minutes for the first 500g (1lb) and then two minutes for each additional 100g (4oz). Drain when cooked and leave to cool.

A crab can also be killed by inserting a thin metal skewer just above its mouth and pushing this to the back of the shell. The claws and body meat can then be removed and steamed or stir-fried.

To prepare a cooked crab
Twist off the legs and pull the claws off the body. Lay the crab on its back, put your hands under the edge of the central part and push upwards until it breaks. Lever the two pieces apart, remove all ten of the spongy grey fronds (known as 'dead men's fingers') and discard. Drain out any excess water from the shell, remove the stomach sac just below the head and discard. Spoon out the soft, brown meat from the shell – this can be used as a spread for sandwiches or toast.

Crack the claws and pincers and take out all the white meat inside, using a skewer to pick it out of the crevices. Cut the crab body in half with a sharp knife, then in half again, and pick out the meat in this with your fingers. If the legs are large enough, snap them in half, discard the thin end, and crack the shell of the thicker part to remove the meat. Before using in a recipe, break the white meat into large flakes, picking it over carefully to remove any shards of broken shell.

To cook a live lobster
As with crabs, lobsters are best bought live and cooked when ready to eat, To do this, freeze the lobster for two hours to render it unconscious, then

drive a heavy, sharp pointed knife through the cross on its head to kill it instantly – this prevents the meat toughening as it cooks. Plunge the lobster into boiling salted water (dissolve 2 tablespoons salt per 950ml/32 fl oz of water) and simmer for 15 minutes per 500g (1lb), adding two minutes for each additional 500g.

Alternatively, the lobster can be cut in half and grilled or the claw and body meat removed and steamed or stir-fried. When cooked the shell turns from its natural dark green or blue-black with orange, brown or red speckles, to a deep brick red.

To prepare a cooked lobster
Twist off the large claws and crack them to remove the flesh. If the smaller claws are large enough, these can be cracked and the meat removed from them as well. Split the lobster down the middle on the underside of the body from head to tail, using a strong, sharp knife. Remove and discard the intestine, which looks like a small vein running through the centre of the tail, the stomach near the head and the grey, spongy gills, none of which are edible. Serve the flesh in the half shells garnished with the cracked claws and legs, or remove the flesh and use in a recipe as required.

To cook live crayfish
Take care when handling live crayfish as, although small, they can still deliver a painful nip. Freeze them for an hour to render them unconscious, then drop into a pan of boiling salted water and cook just long enough for them to turn fiery red and their tails to begin to curl. Drain and peel as soon as they are cool enough to handle, because the longer they are left, the harder the shells will be to remove.

To prepare cooked crayfish
Turn the crayfish over on its back and twist the tail until it cracks. Pull the tail away from the shell, remove the intestinal thread and pick out the meat. Generally only the tail meat is eaten but the heads of small crayfish can be twisted off and the meat sucked out of the shell. The claws of larger crayfish can be cracked to remove any meat.

Oysters

Opening an oyster
Wrap your hand in a tea towel, place the oyster in it, cupped shell down, and steady your hand on the worktop. With the other hand, push the blade of an oyster knife into the hinge of the oyster and firmly work it backwards and forwards into the shell to break the hinge. As it breaks, twist the knife to open the top shell and slide the knife underneath to sever the ligament that attaches the oyster to its shell. Lift off and discard the top shell, keeping the cupped bottom half upright so none of the juices leak out, and pick out any small pieces of shell that have broken off and fallen inside.

If serving oysters on their shells, sit the half shells in crushed ice so they stay upright.

Mussels

Wash the mussels in plenty of cold water, scrape off any barnacles sticking to them and pull out the thread-like beards that mussels use to attach themselves to rocks and other surfaces. Discard any that remain tightly closed after cooking.

Clams and cockles

Wash clams and cockles in plenty of cold water, swirling them around as you do so to rinse away any stubborn grit or sand. The shells can be twisted open by inserting the blade of a small sharp knife on the opposite side to the hinge, but the easiest way to remove the meat is to steam them open in a covered pan with a little water, stock or wine.

Scallops

All scallops need to be washed in plenty of cold water. Unlike the ones that have been dredged, premium diver-caught scallops should be relatively free of sand and grit, but it is worth rinsing them to make sure. Place the scallop on a board, flat shell uppermost, and slide the blade of a filleting knife between the two shells, keeping it flat against the top shell. Once you've located the ligament attaching the meat to the shell, cut through it and the top shell will come away. Remove any debris from the lower cupped shell, leaving just the white muscle meat and the orange coral.

Cuttlefish

Cut off the tentacles in front of the eyes, removing the beak-like mouth from the centre. Cut off the head and discard it, reserving the ink sac if desired. The sac is pearly white with a blue tinge and the ink can be used to flavour pastas and risottos, but take care not to break it accidentally as it will make a dreadful mess. Open the body from top to bottom along the dark-coloured back. Take out the cuttle bone and the intestines and discard. Peel the skin off the body, and also from the tentacles if the cuttlefish is large.

Squid

Carefully pull apart the head and the body. The intestines, including the ink sac, will come away with the head. Reserve the ink sac if desired but discard the head and the rest of the intestines.

Cut off the tentacles in front of the eyes, squeeze out the beak-like mouth in the centre and discard. Pull out the long, plastic-like quill and any soft roe from the body cavity and discard. Peel off the skin from the body and the two side fins and rinse under cold water. The body, the two pieces of muscle running down inside it, the fins and the tentacles can all be eaten.

Octopus

Cut off the tentacles in front of the eyes, press the mouth and beak out from the middle of the tentacles, and discard. Cut off the head at the round openings in the body and discard. Turn the body inside out, pull away the insides and discard, along with the small bone-like strips attached to the sides.

Simmer the body and tentacles very gently in a pan of boiling water for one hour or longer, depending on the size of the octopus, to tenderise it.

Ways to cook fish and shellfish

The quickest way to ruin a beautiful piece of fish or some sweet succulent shellfish is by overcooking, which will turn both from moist and juicy to dry and tasteless in minutes. That said, all fish should be cooked through, except tuna, which is often just seared briefly in a hot pan and, according to personal taste, left rare in the centre.

As a general rule, when pan-frying, grilling, baking or roasting, allow four to five minutes per side for portions of fish 2cm (¾in) thick and a few minutes longer for thicker steaks. If cooking a whole fish on the bone, allow an extra two to three minutes on each side.

To tell if fish is cooked, the flesh should have turned from translucent to opaque and flake easily. For a whole fish, when its eye turns white it is done.

Shellfish need only minimal cooking and will quickly toughen if overdone. Cook raw shrimp until their flesh just turns pink and opaque.

Deep-frying

Ideal for fillets, goujons, smelt, large shrimp and langoustine tails. Because fish and shellfish have such delicate flesh, it is important they are given a protective coating before being deep-fried as this will not only prevent the flesh overcooking and drying out, it will also help it stay moist.

Breadcrumbs, batter or cornmeal all make good coatings for fish and shellfish, either plain or flavoured with herbs, spices or citrus zest. Heat a mild-flavoured oil to 180°C (350°F) and fry until the coating is crisp and golden.

Pan-frying

Good for whole fish, fillets, steaks and scallops. Heat a little oil in a heavy frying pan before adding the fish, and turn over halfway through cooking. Fillets can be dusted in flour seasoned with herbs or spices if you like.

Stir-frying

Suitable for white fish, salmon, scallops, prawns and squid, the fish should be cut into small pieces and added to the pan last as it will cook in just one or two minutes. Firm-fleshed white fish, such as monkfish, is best as it holds its shape when cooked. Softer-fleshed fish needs to be stir-fried carefully.

Steaming

This healthy way to cook fish is widely used in Asian cuisines. Portions or whole fish are placed in a steamer over boiling water or stock, with herbs, spices or other aromatic seasonings added to the liquid or tucked around the fish. Fish can also be wrapped in banana leaves or seaweed before steaming.

Grilling

Best suited to whole fish and firm fillets with a small flake. Also good for oily fish such as mackerel and herring.

Searing and griddling

An excellent way of cooking steaks of fish like salmon, tuna and swordfish is to cook them in a ridged griddle pan, which sears the outside but leaves the centre moist. Heat the pan until very hot before adding the fish and allow the first side to 'seal' before turning over. Good for large prawns and scallops too, but not thin, flaky fillets.

Grilling

Steaks of meaty fish and large prawns are perfect for steeping in a tangy marinade before grilling over charcoal. Small fish like sardines can also be barbecued, either straight over the coals or in a special fish rack to prevent them breaking up.

Poaching

Whole fish and portions can be poached in a mixture of water and wine or lemon juice, or fish stock. If serving cold, poach the fish and then let it cool in the poaching liquid so it stays extra moist. Once cooked the liquid can be used for a sauce or stock.

In stews, soups and braises

All types of fish and shellfish, apart from fish with very oily flesh, can be added to fish stews, soups and braises. Cut the skinned fish into even-sized pieces or chunks and add about five minutes before the end of cooking time, simmering gently until the flesh of the fish or shellfish turns opaque.

Roasting and baking

Because fish overcooks so quickly, take care when baking it in the oven. Whole fish and thick fillets are best for roasting and four different methods can be used: foil-wrapping, en papillote, salt-baking or en croûte.

Microwaving

Only suitable for steaming even-sized portions of fish that are of the same thickness. Place in a single layer on a plate, cover with pierced plastic wrap, and microwave on full power, allowing five minutes per 500g (1lb) of fish.

Smoking

Kits are available for home-smoking oily fish such as mackerel, trout, salmon and herring.

FISH

One of the oldest foods known to mankind, thousands of different species of fish – almost thirty thousand at the last count – swim the world's oceans, lakes and rivers. Some live in salt water, some in fresh, others prefer to migrate between the two. Some are so small they are almost invisible to the naked eye whilst others, such as the giant marlin, are amongst the largest creatures in the world. High in protein, minerals and vitamins but low in fat, fish make a valuable contribution to a healthy diet and can be cooked in virtually any way you choose.
Baked, grilled, fried, barbecued, steamed, braised or made into a pie, the choice is yours. Just two simple rules: buy fish as fresh as possible and don't overcook it or the delicate flesh will dry out and become tough and tasteless.

Witch
(alternative names grey sole, witch flounder)

Glyptocephalus cynoglossus

plie grise (French), mendo (Spanish), passera lingua di cane
(Italian), Rotzunge (German), solhao (Portuguese)

Atlantic halibut

Hippoglossus hippoglossus

flétan (French), hipogloso negro (Spanish), ippogloso
Atlantico (Italian), Heilbutt (German), alabote-de-Atlantico
(Portuguese)

Closely related species: Pacific halibut
Other related species: mock, black, and Greenland
halibut (known as turbot in Canada).

Characteristics Similar
to megrim in looks and
flavour, this flat fish,
known in America as
'grey sole', has pale
brown skin and subtly
flavoured white flesh
that requires careful
cooking or it will dry
out. Traditionally very
popular in France and
Spain – and not just at
Halloween – grey sole
is now finding its way
onto restaurant menus in
other countries as chefs
search for alternative fish
varieties whose stocks
are not endangered.

North Carolina, witch
are mostly trawled as
bycatch with other white
fish, such as haddock
and cod. Slow-growing
and long-lived, they
spawn in spring but it
is three to four years
before they are ready to
reproduce. An average
lifespan is 14 years but
25-year-old witch have
been documented.

Available All year
round. Whole fish.

Cooking Best cooked
on the bone. Grill or
pan-fry.

Habitat Found off
the southwest shores
of England, down the
Atlantic coast of western
Europe and in deep cold
waters from Canada to

Substitute Plaice,
lemon sole, megrim.

Characteristics The
largest flat fish, halibut
can to grow to 300-kilo
giants in the deepest,
coldest waters. Their
white flesh is prized for
its excellent flavour and
firm, meaty texture. The
body has a large mouth
and pointed tail, with
dark, greenish-brown
skin on the eye side and
white skin on the other.
Smaller fish are usually
found in shallower waters
and are known as 'chick',
'chicken' or 'baby'
halibut, while really large
specimens are dubbed
'whales'.

Habitat Strong
swimmers that live on
the seabed in the north
Atlantic, North Sea and
Pacific. Best-quality fish
are caught by line so
the catch is expensive.
Atlantic halibut live
closer inshore than
Pacific halibut and are
now farmed in Norway.

Available Farmed all
year round. Mostly
available as steaks.

Cooking Bake, braise or
poach and serve with a
delicate sauce.

Substitute Turbot, brill.

Plaice

Hippoglossoides platessoides;
Pleuronectes spp.

carrelet, plie (French), *solla* (Spanish), *passera* (Italian),
Scholle, Goldbutt (German), *solha* (Portuguese)

Characteristics A member of the flounder family, ranging in size from 225g (8oz) to 2kg (4½lb). The flesh is black with orange spots on the eye side, and white on the other. Best eaten as fresh as possible as the white, flaky flesh, which has a naturally mild flavour, deteriorates quickly, becoming dull and tasteless. To judge freshness, check the colour of the orange spots, which should be clear and bright.

Habitat As with other flat fish, plaice are seabed dwellers. They are the most abundant flat fish in Europe, where they are caught from the western Mediterranean to Norway. Across the Atlantic, American plaice are caught off the Canadian coast and are the largest flounder catch of that region.

Available All year round. Whole fish and fillets.

Cooking Whole fish: grill, pan-fry, bake. Fillets: fry, grill, poach, steam.

Substitute Lemon sole, megrim, witch, dab, flounder.

Megrim
(alternative names whiff, sail-fluke)

Lepidorhombus whiffiagonis

cardine franche (French), *gallo* (Spanish), *rombo giallo* (Italian), *Scheefschnut, Flugelbutt* (German), *areiro* (Portuguese)

Characteristics From the same family as turbot and brill, megrim has the same oval shape and long frilly dorsal fin as lemon sole but the two are not related. The skin on the eye side is a sandy dark brown and white on the blind side with four black marks on the back of the dorsal fin. Small to medium in size, megrim are best cooked and eaten on the bone as they can be quite dry.

Habitat Caught mainly off the southwest coast of England, the Spanish have more of a taste for megrim than the British, so most end up there. A deeper-water species than most flat fish, it is caught from Britain to Gibraltar and in the Mediterranean. It is known by various names, including rooster and Irish megrim, the latter considered to be superior to the common megrim.

Available All year round. Whole fish.

Cooking Allow a 340–400g (12–14oz) fish per person and pan-fry or grill. Best very fresh.

Substitute Turbot, brill, lemon sole.

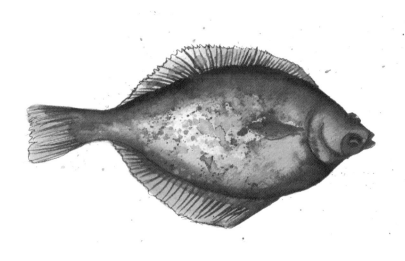

Dab
(alternative names American/Canadian plaice)

Limanda limanda

limande (French), *limanda nordica* (Spanish), *limanda* (Italian), *Scharbe, Kliesche* (German),
solha-escura-do-mar-do-norte (Portuguese)

Characteristics Dab is a small fish and a close relative of the larger, more ubiquitous flounder. The upper eye side of the skin is brown with dark blotches, small speckles and similar orange spots to plaice. Easily identifiable by the strongly arched lateral line that curves in a semi-circle over the pectoral fin, which can be orange, just behind the head. The white flesh is sweet and flaky but needs to be eaten very fresh because it deteriorates quickly.

Habitat Found all around the British Isles and in Scandinavia, dab live on the seabed in sandy areas. Young fish stay inshore, while adults migrate shorewards from deeper water during the summer.

Available Best April to July. Whole. Rarely caught smaller than 700g (1½lb) because the flesh can be bland.

Cooking Grill, pan-fry or steam. In the Jutland area of Denmark, larger sand dab are salted, dried and also smoked.

Substitute Flounder, plaice.

Lemon sole

Microstomus kitt

limande-sole (French), *mendo limon* (Spanish), *sogliola limanda* (Italian), *limande, Echte rotzunge* (German), *solha-limao* (Portuguese), *winter flounder* (US)

Related species: grey, sand, French, Oriental and rex sole

Characteristics More readily available and therefore far more affordable than Dover sole. The white flesh may be softer and more delicate than that of its famous cousin but it still makes excellent eating when served plainly cooked or with a rich sauce. The oval body is more rounded than that of a Dover, and the skin on the dark side a lighter, more yellowy, brown.

Habitat The best lemon sole are said to be those caught off the southwest coast of Britain, and they command the highest price, but large quantities are landed in the North Sea and on the Eastern Seaboard in the US.

Available All year round. Whole fish and fillets.

Cooking Whole fish: grill or fry. Fillets: fry, grill, bake, poach or steam, Fillets can be spread with a stuffing, rolled or folded, and served with a rich sauce.

Substitute Plaice, Dover sole, megrim.

Flounder
(alternative name fluke)

Pleuronectidae

fiet (French), *platija* (Spanish), *passera pianuzza* (Italian), *Flunder, Butt, Struffbutt* (German), *solha-das-pedras* (Portuguese)

*Related species: yellowtail flounder, petrale sole, largetooth flounder,
California halibut, halibut fluke*

Characteristics The most prolific member of the flat fish family with fine, sweet flesh. Adult fish actually swim on their sides and their Latin family name, Pleuronectidae, means 'side swimmer'. North European fish have bright white skin on their blind side and brownish-green on the eye side with faint red spots. Related species vary in colour as, like other flat fish, flounder camouflage themselves by partially burrowing into the sand and changing their skin colour according to their habitat.

Habitat They swim very close to the shore and are found mainly in northern waters around the US,

Canada, Iceland, north Europe, Spain and Portugal.

Available All year round. Whole fish when small around 350g (12 oz), larger fish of 1kg (2lb) and upwards sold as fillets.

Cooking Best cooked simply – pan-fry, grill or steam – and best eaten as fresh as possible as the texture and flavour of the flesh quickly deteriorates.

Substitute Dab, plaice, lemon sole.

Turbot

Psetta maxima

turbot (French), *rodaballo* (Spanish), *rombo chiodato* (Italian), *Steinbutt* (German), *pregado* (Portuguese)

Characteristics More highly prized, and consequently even more expensive, than halibut, turbot has firm, easy-to-handle white flesh and a full flavour. It has a massive body and tiny head. The brown skin on the upper side varies from light to dark brown, is spotted with green or black and studded with more knobbly tubercles than a toad. The blind underside is white. In the wild, turbot range in size from 400g (14oz) to 8kg (18lb) and sometimes more.

Habitat A European fish found from Iceland to the inshore waters of the Mediterranean. Diminishing stocks have led to fish farms being established in recent years in Spain, France, and Chile; farmed fish are distinguished by their lighter skin.

Available Farmed all year round. Wild season April to February. Whole fish weighing around 450g (1lb) are available but they yield too little flesh to be worth buying. Choose a 1.25–1.5kg (2¾–3¼lb) fish to feed four, or steaks from a larger fish.

Cooking Whole fish: bake or poach. Steaks: grill, pan-fry, poach or steam and serve with a light creamy or herb sauce. Best cooked on the bone with the skin on, the gelatinous bones make excellent stock.

Substitute Halibut, brill.

Brill

Scophthalmus rhombus

barbue (French), *remol* (Spanish), *rombo liscio* (Italian), *Glattbutt, Kleist* (German), *rodovalho* (Portuguese)

Characteristics Similar to turbot but smaller and less highly regarded, despite brill having white, succulent flesh. The body is almost oval in shape with a white blind side and grey-brown eye side with light and dark freckles but no tubercles (small, rounded nodules). As with turbot, the skin colour changes according to where the fish is caught, so lighter fish are found on sandy sea floors with darker, richer hued ones on muddier beds. Brill is unusual in that the gap between its eyes is wider than their diameter.

Habitat Lives on the seabed of the shallow, inshore waters of the Mediterranean and as far north as

Norway and Iceland. Brill are not found in the western Atlantic.

Available All year round. Whole (smaller fish weighing less than 450g/1lb). Steaks and fillets from larger fish.

Cooking Fry, poach, sear or bake steaks and fillets. Grill or pan-fry whole fish.

Substitute Turbot, halibut.

Dover sole

Solea solea

sole (French), *lenguado* (Spanish), *sogliola* (Italian), *Seezunge* (German), *linguado* (Portuguese)

Characteristics The king of soles takes its name from the port of Dover on the south coast of the UK and has inspired many classic French dishes from sole meunière to sole bonne femme. Longer and narrower than other flat fish, it has dark brown skin on top that can simply be pulled away before cooking. The thin white skin on the underside is usually left on and eaten. The flesh is snow-white and melt-in-the-mouth when cooked but firm enough when raw for fillets to be rolled or folded around a stuffing without falling apart. Fish straight from the sea are too firm to cook immediately and are considered to be at their best after two or three days, when their texture and flavour is enhanced. Large Dover soles are known as tongues; small ones as slips.

Habitat Once fished in huge quantities in the North Sea and off the southwest coast of England and the Benelux countries but now much rarer. Fish come inshore to spawn in spring.

Available All year round. Fish weighing 400g (14oz) to 450g (1lb) are perfect for serving whole, one per person. Larger fish will give fillets for two people.

Cooking Grill or pan-fry whole fish on the bone. Fry, poach or steam fillets, or roll around a stuffing. Rich sauces go well with the almost sweet flesh.

Substitute Lemon sole.

Wolffish

(alternative names ocean catfish,
seacat, rockfish, lobo)

Anarhichadidae

loup marin (French), *Katfisch* (German), *havkat* (Danish),
zeewolf (Dutch), *steinbitur* (Icelandic)

Characteristics The
long, eel-like body has
smooth, dark blue-
grey skin that can be
spotted or striped and
has primitive scales.
The giant mouth has
two long rows of sharp
teeth on the upper and
lower jaws (from which
the fish gets its name)
for grinding up its diet
of starfish, molluscs and
crustaceans. The flesh
is firm, white and sweet
and holds its shape when
cooked. An average
size is 4.5kg (10lb) but
fish weighing 18kg (40lb)
and more have been
recorded.

Habitat A solitary,
slow-swimming, bottom-

dweller caught across
the Atlantic from France
to Cape Cod and north
to Greenland. Iceland
lands the biggest catch.
Over-fishing has led
to depleted stocks and
spotted wolffish are now
being farmed in Norway.
Another related species
is found in the Pacific.

Available Spring and
summer. Farmed fish
available all year. Whole
fish, fillets and steaks.

Cooking Bake, grill, fry,
poach, steam.

Substitute Cod, other
members of the cod
family, haddock.

Sablefish

(alternative names Alaska black cod,
butterfish, candlefish, coal fish)

Anoplopoma fimbria

morue charbonnière, rascasse noire (French), *bacalao*
negro (Spanish), *merluzzo dell'Alasca* (Italian), *Kohlenfisch*
(German), *gindara* (Japanese)

Characteristics A
premium fish that takes
its name from its black
or dark green skin. The
firm, pearly white flesh
has large, moist flakes
and a superb rich flavour
that is high in omega-3
fatty acids and low in
dioxins and mercury.
Average-sized fish weigh
from 1.4–4.5kg (3–10lb)
and they can be very
long-lived; the oldest
recorded sablefish was
94. Highly prized in
Japan and often called
black cod, despite not
being a member of the
cod family.

Habitat Lives on the
muddy seabed in the

very deep waters of the
Pacific, most abundantly
off the coast of northern
British Columbia and in
the Gulf of Alaska.

Available All year
round. Frozen fillets and
steaks, rarely available
fresh. Also smoked for
sale in Jewish delis.

Cooking Pan-fry, bake,
grill, steam, poach or
braise. In Japan a classic
recipe is sablefish
marinated in sweet miso
for two to three days
before being pan-fried
and finished in the oven.

Substitute Halibut,
monkfish, cod.

Gurnard

Aspitrigla cuculus; Eutrigla gurnardus

grondin (French), *rubios* (Spanish), *capone* (Italian), *Knurrhahn* (German), *cabra* (Portuguese), *sea robin* (US)

Characteristics Common species include the red, grey and yellow or tub gurnard. All have a mild flavour, firm flesh and the same ugly big heads; only their skin colour changes, the most spectacular being the flying gurnard which has brilliant red fins and green, blue and black speckles. Most fish are quite small, commonly 340g (12oz) to 2kg (4½lb), although larger ones weighing 2.5kg (5½lb) are not unknown.

Habitat It was the Greek philosopher Aristotle who first documented the strange, but untranslatable, grunting sounds gurnard make to each other as they drift along the seabed. Still found in Greece as well as the rest of the Mediterranean, they are fished all over the world from Africa and the south Atlantic, to the Black Sea, the Gulf of Mexico and Japan.

Available Spring, summer and autumn. Whole fish and fillets.

Cooking Plenty of bones mean whole fish are mainly used for stocks and soups, in particular bouillabaisse. Fillets can be baked, fried, poached or served in a strong-flavoured sauce.

Substitute Red mullet, grey mullet.

Cusk

(alternative names oyster fish, tusk, ocean whitefish)

Brosme brosme

brosme (French), *brosmio* (Spanish, Italian), *Lumb* (German), *menyok* (Russian)

Characteristics Cusk can grow up to 6.8kg (15lb), although an average size is about 2.25kg (5lb). A long dorsal fin runs the length of the long thin body, giving it the appearance of an eel, and skin colour can vary from brown-red to green-brown or greyish yellow, shading to cream on the belly. Despite a big, whiskered mouth, slimy skin and a strong smell, cusk are good to eat and have firm flesh with a mild, slightly sweet flavour and large flakes that hold together when cooked.

Habitat A slow-growing, solitary swimmer that lives in the northern coastal waters of both the western and eastern Atlantic. Fished from Cape Cod to Newfoundland and off the coasts of Denmark, Murmansk, Norway, Iceland and Scotland.

Available All year round. Whole fish or fillets, fresh or dried, salted and brined.

Cooking Grill, fry, poach or bake. As the flesh stays firm, it is especially good for soups, chowders and kebabs.

Substitute Cod, haddock.

Grenadier

(alternative name rattail)

Coryphaenoides spp.

grenadier (French), *grenadero* (Spanish), *granatiere* (Italian), *Grenadierfisch* (German), *granadeiro* (Portuguese)

Characteristics A gigantic head and skinny, pointed tail won't win the grenadier many fans in an aquatic beauty pageant but its firm, succulent flesh, which can be as thick as 2.5cm (1in) at the head end but wafer-thin at the tail, is sweet, pure white and has a good flavour. Commonly 30–60cm (1–2ft) in length, its sharp scales and coarse grey skin made filleting hard, until an industrial process was developed.

Habitat Trawled mainly in the deep waters off Atlantic Canada, as well as along the Pacific coast of the US. Different species of grenadier can be found from the Arctic to the Antarctic. Living at great depths by day (4,500m/15,000ft), grenadier rise into shallower waters at night.

Available All year round. Fillets – the sharply tapering tail means the flesh yield is only about 20 per cent

Cooking Fry, bake or use in hearty soups such as chowders

Substitute Any member of the cod family or a firm-fleshed white fish such as monkfish.

Weakfish
(alternative names grey sea trout, corvina, spotted sea trout)

Cynoscion regalis

accoupa pintade (French), *corvinata pintada* (Spanish, Portuguese), *ombrina dentata* (Italian), *Gefleckter umberfisch* (German), *squeateague* (American Indian)

Characteristics The weakfish has deep olive-green skin with purple, blue or coppery tints, small dark speckles on its back and sides and a white belly. With flesh that is flaky and moist, it is delicious fresh but deteriorates quickly. A powerful swimmer and strong fighter, anglers coined the name 'weakfish' because slack mouth muscles often enable a fish to break free of a hook. The market weight is around 1kg (2lb) but larger specimens can weigh up to 13.5kg (30lb).

Habitat Fished off the Eastern Seaboard of America during the summer months from Nova Scotia to north Florida.

Available Summer. Whole fish, fillets.

Cooking The finest way to cook a whole fish is said to be to stuff the body cavity with crab, wrap it in foil, and bake. Can also be fried, grilled or served with a light sauce.

Substitute Cod, haddock, bluefish.

Patagonian toothfish
(alternative names icefish, toothfish, Antarctic sea bass, Chilean sea bass)

Dissostichus eleginoides

Characteristics A relative newcomer to the market. Similar to sea bass, with white, firm flesh that has a high oil content but is less delicately flavoured. Slow-growing with sunken eyes, smoky green skin and large pectoral fins, an average fish should weigh around 9kg (20lb) but over-fishing and illegal catches have resulted in smaller fish and depleted stocks. Too many fish being caught before they reach their spawning age of eight years have caused many restaurants and shoppers to boycott Patagonian toothfish until stocks recover.

Habitat Lives solely in southern oceans off South Georgia, the Falklands and around the tip of South America from Argentina to Chile.

Available All year round. Usually sold frozen as skinless steaks or fillets, under the name Chilean sea bass.

Cooking Bake, grill, pan-fry or braise. Avoid deep-frying or serving with a rich sauce as the flesh is too oily.

Substitute Cod.

Cod

Gadus spp.

cabillaud (French), *bacalao* (Spanish), *merluzzo bianco* (Italian), *Kabeljiau, Dorsch* (German),

bacalhau-do-Atlantico (Portuguese)

Characteristics A superb white fish with a long tapered body and silvery skin, mottled sandy brown and greyish green with dark speckles. Giant cod of 50kg (112lb) or more once cruised the oceans but today 6–7kg (13–15lb) is considered large. Smaller fish of 450g–2kg (1–4lb) are known as codling, the Canadian tomcod being a related species.

Habitat Caught in both the Atlantic and Pacific, preferably by line as netting and trawling can bruise the cod's delicate, pure white flesh. Icelandic fishermen say the best cod has 'snow in its mouth', as very cold water helps firm up its flesh.

Available All year round. Smaller fish are sold as fillets. Bigger fish give meatier steaks with large, succulent flakes.

Cooking Very versatile, cod can be grilled, fried, poached and baked or added to stews, soups and pies. The sweet flesh will take most flavours but requires care as it is easily overcooked.

Substitute Other members of the cod family: haddock, hake, whiting, cusk, grenadier.

Kingklip
(alternative names ling, cusk eel)

Genypterus spp.

abadèche (French), *abadejo* (Spanish), *abadeco* (Italian), *Schlangenfisch* (German),
congrio (Latin America), *kingu* (Japanese), *cusk eel* (UK)

Characteristics Long and slender with slimy skin, this eel-like fish is rich in both omega-3 and omega-6 fatty acids. Of its four species – red, golden, black and South African – the golden and red are considered to have the superior texture and flavour, their pink flesh turning pure white when cooked. The black kingklip has darker flesh and thinner fillets and can be identified by yellow spots on its skin. The South African kingklip has firm white flesh with a mild flavour. Adult fish can grow to 1.8m (6ft) in length and weigh up to 23kg (50lb), although 4.5kg (10lb) is the average.

Habitat Fished in deep water off the coasts of Chile, Argentina and South Africa, the southwest Pacific off New Zealand, and the temperate waters of Australia, the kingklip's habitat can vary from rocky ground to soft sand and mud, into which it burrows.

Available All year round although stocks are lighter in winter. Large and small fillets (450g–2kg/1–4lb).

Cooking Grill, steam, fry, poach or bake. The dense flesh holds its shape when cooked so is a good choice for fish soups, including the Chilean speciality caldillo congrio, a hearty fish soup similar to bouillabaisse.

Substitute Orange roughy, sea bass, monkfish, ling.

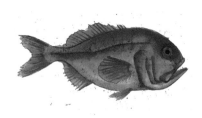

Orange roughy

Hoplostethus atlanticus

empereur, hoplostète rouge (French), *reloj* (Spanish), *pesce specchio Atlantico* (Italian), *Granatbarsch* (German), *olho-de-vidro-laranja* (Portuguese)

Characteristics
This fish was restyled 'orange roughy' when fishermen recognised its marketing potential but knew the original name, slimehead, would attract few customers. Whole fish weigh around 1.5kg (3½lb), have bright orange skin, big bony heads and pointed fins. The large-flaked, pearly white flesh becomes opaque when cooked and has a delicate flavour. The darker the flesh the less good it is to eat.

Habitat It was thought to be only found in the seas south of Iceland, but in the 1970s specimens

were discovered between Tasmania and New Zealand. A deep-water habitat and 40-year reproduction cycle make responsible fishing imperative.

Available All year round. Always sold as fillets. Whole fish have a layer of orange-brown fat under the skin that is a powerful laxative – this is removed in filleting.

Cooking Bake, grill or poach and serve with a light sauce rather than fry as the flesh is moderately oily.

Substitute Hake, cod.

Hoki

(alternative names whiptail, blue hake, New Zealand whiting, blue grenadier)

Macruronus novaezelandia

hoki, merlu à longue queue (French), *merluza azul* (Spanish), *nasello azzurro* (Italian), *Langschwanz-seehect* (German), *granadeiro-azul* (Portuguese)

Characteristics Long and tapering with the dorsal and anal fins converging at a pointed tail, New Zealand whiting have big hake-like mouths, sharp pointed teeth and tiny scales. Growing up to 1.2m (1ft) long, these fish can live for 25 years. Their skin is pale blue-green and their flesh white with a mild flavour and few bones.

Habitat Deep-sea dwellers where they feed on lantern fish, squid and crustaceans. Caught around New Zealand,

South Africa and off the Chilean coast at depths of up to 4,500m (15,000ft). Over-trawling has led to depleted stocks.

Available All year round. Almost always frozen as long skinned fillets.

Cooking Fry, bake, poach or serve with a rich sauce.

Substitute Cod, haddock or another white fish.

Haddock

Melanogrammus aeglefinus

aiglefin, anon, eglefin (French), *eglefino* (Spanish), *asinello* (Italian), *Schellfisch* (German), *arinca* (Portuguese)

Characteristics Similar to cod but not as big, an average-size haddock weighs around 1.8kg (4lb). Smaller fish weighing 700–900g (1½–2lb) are known as scrod in New England and Canada. The flesh is not as white or as flaky as cod's but has a slightly sweeter taste, making haddock the best white fish for smoking. Above the pectoral fin, the greyish brown skin is marked with a black smudge, similar to that on a John Dory.

Habitat Usually trawled, but can also be line caught, in the cold waters off Norway, Iceland and Russia, as well as on both sides of the north Atlantic.

Available All year round. Sold as fillets, haddock are too small for good-size steaks or cutlets.

Cooking Scotland's number-one choice for its famous battered fish and chip suppers, haddock can also be pan-fried, grilled, poached or steamed and made into soups, stews and pies. When poaching, the skin should be left on so the flesh holds together.

Substitute Cod and other members of the cod family.

Whiting

Merlangius merlangus

merlan (French), *merlan* (Spanish), *merlano* (Italian), *Wittling, Merlan* (German), *badejo* (Portuguese)

Characteristics Like hake, whiting has a reputation for flabby, bland flesh, but eaten really fresh with a rich, buttery sauce it can be very good. A small member of the cod family, but more slender than both cod and haddock, the upper half of the body has a golden, olive-green hue, while the sides and belly are bluish white, with a pale brown lateral line separating the two. The fragile flesh needs careful handling, has a small flake, and rapidly loses texture and flavour if not eaten on the day it is purchased, or if overcooked.

Habitat Caught all around the British Isles where it lives in shoals over sand or sandy mud and gravel and feeds in mid-to-bottom waters at depths of between 18 and 140m (60 and 450ft). Also caught in the northwest Atlantic and the Pacific.

Available All year round. Whole fish, fillets.

Cooking Fry, bake or grill and serve with a rich sauce. Good in fish mousses and fishcakes.

Substitute Hake, cod, haddock.

Hake

Merluccius spp.

merlu, merluchon, or chon/merlan (small/large Mediterranean) (French), *merluza* (Spanish),
nasello (Italian), *Seehecht* (German), *pescada* (Portuguese)

Characteristics Long and slender with silvery blue skin and a slate-grey back, the carnivorous hake has a large head with numerous sharp, curved teeth. Small hake feed on krill, graduating to octopus and other fish as they grow. The soft, mild-flavoured flesh is often dismissed as watery and rather coarse, but it firms up on cooking. Highly regarded in Spain, Portugal and Italy, a significant proportion of hake caught in UK waters is exported to those countries, where fish lovers pay premium prices.

Habitat Caught in both Europe and the US, hake prefer the ocean bed by day but move nearer the surface at night to feed. Related species are found off the coasts of Argentina, Chile, Peru, southern Africa and Antarctica.

Available All year round. Small fish weighing 450–900g (1–2lb) are best on the bone; larger fish and related species such as white hake, Cape hake and Capensis hake can be cut into steaks or fillets.

Cooking Bake, grill, fry, poach or steam.

Substitute Cod and other members of the cod family.

Ocean sunfish
(alternative name mola mola)

Mola mola
mambo fish (Taiwan), *fan-che pufferfish* (China)

Characteristics The largest of the numerous varieties of sunfish, this relative of the pufferfish can be blue, silver-grey or white. It is also the largest of all bony fish and can grow to 2m (6ft) in length and weigh in at a massive 1,000kg (2,200lb). 'Mola', its alternative name, is Latin for millstone, an appropriate way to describe its round, very flattened shape, blunt head and almost-not-there tail.

Habitat Found in all oceans of the world, apart from the polar Arctic and Antarctic seas, ocean sunfish live on the surface and are often mistaken for sharks, as their dorsal fin protrudes above the waves.

Frequently trapped as bycatch in illegal gillnets, landing ocean sunfish is banned in the EU.

Available Of no great commercial value in most parts of the world as its bony flesh is considered inedible and can contain high levels of dangerous toxins. It is greatly prized, however, in Taiwan, Japan and Korea.

Cooking Every part of the fish is eaten in Southeast Asia, including the fins and guts.

Substitute None.

Ling

Molva molva

lingue, julienne (French), *maruca* (Spanish), *molva* (Italian), *Leng, Lengfisch* (German), *maruca* (Portuguese)

Characteristics Similar to the kingklip, another long, thin member of the cod family that can grow up to 1.5m (5ft) in length. Adult fish have brown skin tinged with bronze and greenish brown marks and a white belly, while younger fish are yellow/olive green with a lilac hue. The scale-free skin is marked with a dark patch at the back of both dorsal fins, and below the large mouth, on the chin, is a single barbel. The white flesh is firm-textured and has a good flavour that marries well with strong flavours.

Habitat A north Atlantic dweller living in very deep water around the coasts of Scotland, southwest Ireland, Iceland and in the North Sea. Because ling prefer rocky ground they are seldom trawled and are mostly line-caught. Adult fish inhabit heavy rock formations or big wrecks; younger smaller fish are found closer inshore in shallow, rocky water. A single female can lay up to 60 million eggs. Other species of ling such as the rock ling and pink ling are found in the southern hemisphere.

Available All year round. Fillets, both fresh and salted and dried.

Cooking Bake, grill, fry, poach or steam. Because ling have few bones they are particularly good in a fish pie.

Substitute Cod, hake, pollock.

Grey mullet

Mugilidae spp.

mulet, muge (Mediterranean) (French), *lisa, mujol* (Spanish), *cefalo, muggine* (Italian),
Meerasche (German), *tainha, mugem* (Portuguese)

Characteristics Over 100 species of mullet exist worldwide but grey is considered the best. No relation to red mullet, it ranges in size from 450g (1lb) to 1.6kg (3½lb), although lesser species can weigh up to 2.75kg (6lb) or more. Similar in appearance to sea bass but with larger scales, the flesh is firm and juicy and ideal for cooking with strong flavours. The roe is highly prized for taramasalata, poutargue and bottarga and is eaten smoked in Florida.

Habitat Caught in the open sea, grey mullet are excellent but once fish drift inshore to feed, their flesh can taste muddy. Coastal lagoons provide a good supply in the Mediterranean.

Available Spring and summer. As whole fish and fillets. Once scaled, the skin can be left on.

Cooking Bake, grill and fry.

Substitute Sea bass.

Pollock

Pollachius pollachius

lieu jaune, colin jaune (French), *abadejo* (Spanish), *merluzzo giallo* (Italian), *Pollack* (German), *juliana* (Portuguese)

Characteristics A member of the cod family, but a smaller fish, growing to only 25–75cm (10–30in) in length, with large eyes, a big mouth and protruding bottom lip. Its grey-green skin has a golden sheen, tiny scales and a lateral green-brown line curving down each side. Its flesh, which has an excellent flavour, breaks into large white flakes when cooked.

Habitat Dwindling supplies of cod have persuaded more and more chefs and home cooks to put the greener pollock on their menus. Living in abundance around the shores of southwest England, Brittany and the west of Ireland, it prefers to be out at sea in deep water, although younger ones can be found in kelp beds closer inshore and around reefs, rocks, pier walls and wrecks.

Available All year round, although winter availability varies. Small whole fish, fillets.

Cooking Fry, bake, steam, grill and poach, or use in fish pies and casseroles.

Substitute Cod, haddock, hake and ling.

Coley
(*alternative names saithe, coalfish, Atlantic pollock*)

Pollachius virens

lieu noir, colin noir (French), *carbonero* (Spanish), *merluzzo nero* (Italian),

Seelachs, Kohler (German), *escamudo* (Portuguese)

Characteristics Long and tapered with a blue-green skin that shades to charcoal, hence the alternative name of coalfish. Coley range in size from 450g–6kg (1–13lb) and are a distant relative of the Alaskan pollock (see page 57). If eaten very fresh it is delicious, but the flesh, which has a dull, off-white tinge (that lightens during cooking), can quickly acquire a greyish hue and lose texture and flavour.

Habitat Found in the north Atlantic around the UK, particularly the north of Scotland, Ireland, Iceland and Scandinavia. Coley spend the winter in deep water but move shorewards in spring.

Available All year round. Usually they are only available as fillets.

Cooking Any recipe calling for cod or haddock can be adapted for coley. In Bergen, Norway, where wildly flapping, live coley are a familiar sight in the market, they are the main ingredient in the local speciality, fish soup.

Substitute Cod, haddock and other members of the cod family.

Rascasse
(alternative name scorpionfish)

Scorpaena spp.

rascasse, chapon (Provence) (French), *cabracho, rascacio*
(Spanish), *escorpa roja* (Catalan), *scorfano* (Italian),
Drachenkopfe (German), *rascasso,*
cantarilho (Portuguese)

Ocean perch

Sebastes spp.

sebaste, dorade sebaste, rascasse du nord (French), *gallineta*
nordica (Spanish), *sebaste, scorfano di Norvegia* (Italian),
Rotbarsch, Goldbarsch (German), *cantarilho, peixe vermelho*
(Portuguese), *arasuka sake, menuke* (Japanese)

Characteristics An
essential ingredient in
a bouillabaisse. Also
known as scorpionfish,
the name could not be
more appropriate as it
has an array of poisonous
spines that remain active
even after it is dead.

Habitat Traditionally a
Mediterranean fish, two
varieties of rascasse, red
and black, are caught in
nets by small boats off
Mediterranean shores.
However, global warming
has drawn rascasse
farther north and some
have been spotted in
French and British

waters. Scorpionfish
are caught on both the
east and west coasts
of the US, notably the
California scorpionfish
(*Scorpaena guttata*).

Available All year
round. Whole fish
and fillets.

Cooking The bones and
fillets of small fish are
used for making soups
and stocks. Larger fish,
around 1.4kg (3lb), can
be baked or fried whole.

Substitute Red snapper,
gurnard, monkfish,
halibut, cusk, coley.

Characteristics All
species of ocean perch
are slow-growing and
easy to catch. An
average fish weighs
700–900g (1½–2lb),
has red-gold skin, small
spines on its head and
sharp fins on the upper
body. The flesh is flaky,
white and delicately
flavoured.

Habitat Originally a
major catch landed
mainly in the US and
Canada, and at large
north European ports.
As worldwide demand
for fish grew and stocks
became depleted in

Europe, New Zealand
began trawling for ocean
perch, and closely
related species were
discovered in other
deep waters.

Available All year
round. Mostly frozen,
as fillets; whole fish are
sometimes available.

Cooking Fry, bake,
steam, poach, or braise.
Makes good stock.

Substitute Cod,
haddock.

Amberjack
(alternative name yellowtail)

Seriola spp.

seriole (French), *serviola, pez limon* (Spanish), *ricciola* (Italian), *Gelbschwanz, Bernsteinfisch* (German),
esmoregal, charuteiro (Portuguese), *hamachi, buri* (Japanese)

**Related species: *greater amberjack, lesser amberjack, banded rudderfish, Japanese amberjack/
yellowtail, California yellowtail, five-ray yellowtail, flat amberjack***

Characteristics One of many members of the big amberjack family is the greater amberjack, distinguished by dark stripes running from its nose to just in front of its dorsal fin. This large fish can weigh in at around 18kg (40lb), dwarfing the lesser amberjack, which usually tips the scales at under 5kg (11lb). The latter has olive-green or brownish black skin, silver sides and a dark band running upward from its eyes. Another member, the small banded rudderfish, is vertically striped, although larger ones measuring over 25cm (10in) have no bands at all but a raccoon-stripe on the eyes and an iridescent gold strip on each side. The yellowtail is pink-hued and has a yellow band running the length of its body. The flesh of all species of amberjack is rich, fatty and full flavoured.

Habitat Different species live around the world in both cold and warm waters. The greater amberjack is found in rocky reefs around the Balearic Islands but, as with the lesser amberjack and banded rudderfish, is really an Atlantic fish, the banded rudderfish being caught as far north as Nova Scotia. The yellowtail is native to the northwest Pacific from Japan to Hawaii and is much appreciated in Japan, where it is farmed.

Availability All year round. Small fish: whole. Large fish: fillets.

Cooking Grill, bake or fry. The Japanese use the yellowtail's fine-flavoured, firm flesh for sushi.

Substitute Tuna, mackerel.

Black-banded trevally
(alternative names black-banded amberjack, blackbanded kingfish)

Seriolina nigrofasciata

pla sam lee (Thai), *cheung-kung* (Cantonese), *aiburi* (Japanese), *l'amoureuse petit* (Reunion), *seriole amourez* (Djibouti)

Characteristics Growing to a maximum length of 70cm (2¼ft) but more commonly around 40cm (1¼ft), this member of the amberjack family has dusky grey or olive-brown skin on its back and sides and a silvery grey belly. Young fish are banded with wide black diagonal stripes on their upper body. Its local names in French-speaking territories of the Indian Ocean such as Reunion and Djibouti proclaim it as a food of love. Popular in Thailand where its local name is 'cotton fish', due to its soft, bright white flesh.

Habitat Found from the Red Sea through the Indian Ocean to East and South Africa and Indonesia to Thailand, Japan and Australia.

Available All year round. Fillets. Usually fresh but in Hong Kong the flesh is less highly regarded and it is most often salted.

Cooking Deep-fry, pan-fry, grill, bake.

Substitute Snapper, sole.

Alaskan pollock
(alternative names bigeye or walleye cod, Pacific tomcod, Pacific pollock)

Theragra chalcogramma

colin, lieu de l'Alaska (French), *abadejo* (Spanish), *merluzzo dell'Alasca* (Italian), *escamudo do Alasca* (Portuguese)

Characteristics A white fish with flaky flesh that is distantly related to the coley but has a milder, less oily flavour. Sustainability makes pollock the largest food-fish resource on earth and it is a sight on chain restaurant menus worldwide. The sides are marked by a silver line running from head to tail, the skin above the line being greenish black and white below around the belly. Fish can weigh as little as 500–700g (1–1½lb) but can grow into 20kg (46lb) monsters.

Habitat Found over rocks in deep water from Alaska to California, and across the north Pacific to Japan.

Available Season runs from July to September and from December to April. Available frozen all year round. Whole small fish or fillets.

Cooking Grill, fry, steam or bake.

Substitute Cod, haddock, hake.

Surgeonfish

Acanthurus spp.

buntana (India), *labahita* (Philippines), *osuji-kurohagi* (Japanese),
pla khee tang bet lai (Thai), *ngau maan* (Hong Kong)

Characteristics Many different species of surgeonfish exist but two of the most commonly seen have either dark brown or pale blue leathery skin marked with numerous blue lines running down its sides. The white flesh is dense, quite coarse in texture and filling to eat, but has a good flavour.

Habitat Caught from the Red Sea to South Africa, from Japan to Australia's Great Barrier Reef and Micronesia, off the coast of Hawaii and in the Atlantic. It is a popular fish in Southeast Asia, particularly the Philippines.

Available All year round. Whole fish, around 200g to 2kg (7oz to 4½lb), and fillets.

Cooking Whole fish can be pan-fried, grilled or wrapped in foil or banana leaves and roasted or barbecued. Fillets from larger fish can be fried, grilled or steamed. Goes well with a sauce or salsa – particularly Cantonese sweet and sour sauce.

Substitute Grouper, jack/trevally.

Pomfret

Brama spp.

castagnole du Pacifique (French), *palometa, castaneta* (Spanish), *pesce castagna* (Italian),
Brachsenmakrele (German), *capelo, xaputa* (Portuguese)

Characteristics A thin, round-shaped fish with black or silver skin, usually weighing around 450g (1lb). The white, pale silver-skinned variety is one of the most highly prized fish in Indian cuisine, its fine, succulent flesh being easily separated from the bones and marrying well with spicy seasonings. The black pomfret is less highly esteemed but still good to eat and is one of the few species to have decorated a North Vietnamese mail stamp.

Habitat Swimming in Asian coastal waters, the white pomfret is found from the Arabian Gulf, east to Indonesia and north to Japan. The black pomfret is more common in Indonesian waters, particularly around the Philippines, but it ranges from East Africa to southern Japan and Australia. Silver and white pomfret are fished in American waters.

Available All year round. Small whole fish, fillets from larger fish.

Cooking Grill, pan-fry, poach or steam. In India, a favourite way of cooking is to score the skin and coat the fish in strong curry spices before frying, baking or steaming.

Substitute Butterfish, bream.

Black sea bass
(alternative name blackfish)

Centropristis striata
fantre noir d'Amérique (French), *serrano estriado* (Portuguese, Spanish),
perchia striata (Italian), *Schwarzer sägebarsch* (German)

Characteristics A type of grouper found in the US, with lean, fairly firm flesh that has a delicate flavour and small white flakes. Although black, it can adjust its colour to blend into its habitat, shading to grey, brown or dark indigo. The sides are banded with dark vertical lines, and black edges bordering the silver scales give the skin the appearance of being meshed in a fine net.

Habitat Caught from Maine to northeast Florida and in the eastern Gulf of Mexico, it is particularly abundant off the coast of the mid-Atlantic states.

Living close to the sea floor, black sea bass can be found inshore in bays and sounds as well as offshore in deeper water, usually around rocks, reefs, piers and jetties.

Available From September to March. Small fish sold whole weighing 700–900g (1½–2lb), fillets from larger fish (up to 2.25kg/5lb).

Cooking Whole fish and fillets: fry, steam, bake.

Substitute Sea bass.

Milkfish

(alternative name false trevally)

Chanos chanos

ikan susu, lemahan (India), *bangus* (Philippines), *akuta-uo* (Japanese), *pla* (sab) *knanun* (Thai), *hoi lin* (Hong Kong)

Characteristics This native of Southeast Asia is pale blue-grey above and silvery below with a black spot on its shoulder. The tail fin is black edged and the other fins pale yellow. The national symbol of the Philippines, cooks there solve the problem of an excess of bones by gently pounding the fish to loosen the flesh and bones and then pushing the insides out through the mouth. The flesh is made into a stuffing and put back into the skin.

Habitat Shoals gather around shores and islands with coral reefs in the Indian and Pacific Oceans. Young fish migrate to mangrove swamps and estuaries before returning to the sea when large enough to spawn. Fry are also collected from rivers and raised in ponds or lakes.

Available All year. Whole fish and fillets, fresh, frozen, canned, salted and smoked.

Cooking Fry, steam or poach.

Substitute Snapper, bream.

Dorab

(alternative name wolf herring)

Chirocentrus dorab

oki-iwashi (Japanese), *pla dap lao, pla fak pra* (Thai), *parang-parang* (Malaysian), *po do* (Hong Kong)

Characteristics A warm-water relative of the Atlantic herring with an elongated body and large upturned jaws filled with long, dagger-like teeth. Covered in small scales, the back is blue fading to grey with bright silver sides and a sharply forked tail. The dorsal fin is edged in black, distinguishing it from its near twin, the white-fin wolf herring. The flesh has a good flavour but is extremely bony – the Hong Kong Chinese get over this disadvantage by using it for fish balls.

Habitat Found inshore, often in brackish waters, from the Red Sea and East Africa to the Solomon Islands and Tonga, north to the southern shores of Japan and south to Australia's northern coast.

Available All year round but stocks have become depleted due to over-fishing. Fillets and steaks, fresh, frozen or dried and salted.

Cooking Grill, bake, pan-fry or hot smoke.

Alternatives Herring, mackerel.

Sea bass

Dicentrarchus labrax

bar (north and west), *loup de mer* (Mediterranean) (French), *lubina* (Spanish), *branzino*, *spigola* (Italian),
Zachenbarsch (German), *robalo* (Portuguese)

Characteristics The European cousin of the striped American bass has been a highly rated fish since Roman times. Wild, line-caught fish have the finest flavour and texture, but farmed bass are excellent too, with firm, mild tasting white flesh free from small bones. Wild fish have mottled charcoal grey and silver skin, while farmed, which are smaller and usually weigh 300g (10½oz) to 575g (1¼lb), have lighter, more silvery skins.

Habitat Found in the wild from Norway and Iceland to the Mediterranean, where they can grow to over 8kg (17½lb) and are a prize catch. Growing demand, extortionate prices and the threat of depleted stocks have seen fish farms established in Norway and the Mediterranean, particularly Greece and Italy.

Available Farmed fish all year round. Wild fish, spring and summer. Whole fish, fillets and supremes from larger fish.

Cooking After scaling, the skin is good to eat. Whole fish: pan-fry, grill, bake, stuff and bake, steam or poach. Fillets: pan-fry, grill, bake, steam or poach. Excellent both plainly cooked and with Asian spices and herbs such as lemongrass, ginger, coriander and fresh chilli.

Substitute Gilthead bream, barramundi, striped American bass.

Weever fish

Echiichthys vipera, Trachinus spp.

vive (French), *escorpion* (Spanish), *dragone* (Italian), *Petermann,*
Petermannchen (German), *peixhe-aranha* (Portuguese)

Characteristics It may appear pretty harmless but any swimmer stung by the poisonous spines of a weever fish can look forward to several hours of agony. Weevers spend most of their time buried in sand in warm, shallow water rather than swimming, only occasionally emerging to wobble around before disappearing back down with just their venomous black triangular fin exposed. Despite this, their tasty, succulent flesh is very good to eat and the fearsome fins are fortunately usually cut off before they are sold.

Habitat Weevers thrive in the warm shallow waters along the sandy beaches of the south coasts of England and Wales.

Available Spring/summer. Whole fish, weighing 200–300g (7–11oz).

Cooking Barbecue, grill, bake and pan-fry. Excellent for fish soups or stews.

Substitute Rascasse, sea bream, red mullet.

Grouper

Epinephelinae

merou noir (French), *garoupa*, *mero* (Spanish), *cernia* (Italian), *Zackenbarsch* (German),
mero (Portuguese), *rophos* (Greek), *hata, mero* (Japanese)

Species and alternative names: red grouper, black grouper, wreckfish, coney (West Indies),
coral or rock cod (Australia), Malabar grouper (Red Sea), blue-spotted grouper (West Africa),
jewfish, giant hawkfish (Pacific)

Characteristics Related to sea bass, these large – sometimes very large – fish have thick skin, meaty-white flesh with few bones, and a good flavour. Red grouper look spectacular with vivid red-gold skin dotted with blue or yellow spots. Black grouper can range in colour from pale grey to smoky brown and are patterned with paler squiggles and black splodges. Carnivorous, their big mouths have an upturned protruding upper lip and a permanently grumpy expression.

Habitat A solitary fish found around rocks and reefs in shallow tropical, sub-tropical and temperate waters around the world, from the Mediterranean and Africa, to the Caribbean, Gulf of Mexico, South and Central America and the Pacific and Indian Oceans.

Available All year round. Smaller fish (up to about 3kg/6½lb) sold whole, larger ones as fillets or steaks, usually skinned, because the skin is tough and unpleasant to eat. Red grouper is considered to be slightly superior to black.

Cooking Fry, grill (as fillets or kebabs), 'blacken' Cajun-style or use in fish soups and stews. Spices and herbs enhance its flavour.

Substitute Large sea bass.

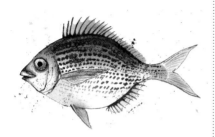

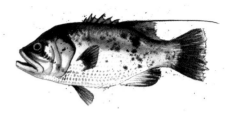

Mojarra
(alternative names silver biddy, whipfish, ponyfish)

Gerreidae

kapas besar (India), *malakapas* (Philippines), *itohikisagi* (Japanese), *pla dok mak* (Thai)

Characteristics A cheap, plentiful fish with numerous related species that can be good when really fresh. Small and silvery with dark blue-grey horizontal blotches on its sides, its second dorsal fin becomes longer and longer as it grows. An average size is 15–20cm (6–8in), although it can grow to 35cm (14in). A bony fish with white, mild-flavoured, meaty flesh that flakes easily when cooked.

Habitat Lives in coastal areas and inshore estuaries where it probably goes to escape from larger predators. Common in the Caribbean and South America, it is also found from East Africa to Japan and down to Australia. Mojarra is its Latin American name; in New South Wales it becomes silver biddy and in the Indian Ocean, ponyfish.

Available Year-round. Whole, frozen and fresh.

Cooking Steam, fry, grill, bake, roast whole or barbecue.

Substitute Bream, snapper, tilapia.

Dhufish
(alternative name dhuie)

Glaucosoma hebraicum

Characteristics Highly regarded for its sweet, creamy flesh and firm, flaky white fillets, this solid, deep-bodied reef fish has big silvery bronze scales and a mauve sheen over its body and head. A black stripe is frequently seen across the eye and males, but not females, have a long filament trailing from their dorsal fin. Most average 4–8kg (9–18lb) in weight, although much larger fish have been caught. To conserve stocks a minimum landing length of 50cm (20in) has been imposed.

Habitat Native to Western Australia, where it is a popular sport fish as well as a commercial fish, this reef- and cave-dweller is usually found in deep water but moves to shallower areas during the cooler months.

Available All year round. Fillets.

Cooking Fry, poach, steam, grill or bake. Its flesh needs careful handling to remain in prime condition and fillets are best cooked simply.

Substitute Halibut, barramundi, any firm white fish.

Bluenose bass

(alternative names blue-eye trevalla, big-eye trevalla, blue-eye cod, blue-nose warehou, bonita, Antarctic butterfish)

Hyperoglyphe antarctica

Characteristics Snub-nosed with a stout body and small scales, the bluenose bass has light-coloured, mild-tasting flesh, with large flakes when cooked. Firm enough when raw for sashimi, Japan is a growing export market, as is the US, where it is beginning to appear on restaurant menus. A bluenose bass can weigh up to 4.5kg (10lb).

Habitat First caught in the early 1950s off the coast of Tasmania and now fished on continental shelves in South Australia, New Zealand, South Africa and Argentina as well.

In New Zealand and Australia, management agencies are introducing quotas to conserve stocks. Adults live near the ocean floor.

Available All year round, but more common during the southern hemisphere's summer months. Whole fish (heads removed and gutted) and skinless fillets, fresh and frozen.

Cooking Fry, grill, bake, sauté, poach, steam or use in a fish soup.

Substitute Sea bass, black sea bass.

Wrasse

Labridae

labre, vieille, coquette (French), *merlo, tordo, gallano* (Spanish), *labridi* (Italian), *Lippfisch* (German), *bodiao* (Portuguese)

Characteristics About 450 species of wrasse live around the world, mostly in warm and tropical waters. Ballan wrasse is a rather coarse-fleshed fish eaten in Scotland and Ireland; California sheephead is large but very good to eat; while tsing ye is an Asian wrasse much enjoyed in China. Generally not highly rated today – but it does make excellent fish soup.

Habitat Ballan wrasse range from Norway to the Mediterranean, floral wrasse from East Africa through Southeast Asia to the western Pacific

and northern Australia. Other species are caught in shallow warm waters around Central and South America and along the Pacific coast of Mexico and California.

Available All year round, with regional variations such as spring/summer for ballan wrasse. Whole fish and fillets, depending on size.

Cooking Bake, pan-fry, steam, poach or use for fish soups and stews.

Substitute Sea bream, rascasse, sea bass.

Barramundi
(alternative names giant sea perch, silver perch)

Lates calcarifer

perca gigante (Spanish), *lates* (Polish, Russian), *kakap, kanja* (India – called *cock-up* by Europeans living in India),
akame (Japanese), *pla kaphong khao* (Thai), *maan cho, mang ts'o* (Hong Kong)

Characteristics A relative of the perch and native to Australia, where 'barramundi' is its Aboriginal name. Long-bodied with golden brown skin above and silvery below, it has brown fins and small eyes – its Hong Kong name translates as 'blind sea bass'. The pearly-white flesh is moist, chunky and has a delicate, highly esteemed flavour. Large game fish of 54kg (120lb) or more are not unknown but an average size is 5.4kg (12lb).

Habitat Found off the eastern shores of the Arabian Gulf through the Indian Ocean to northern Australia, into the Pacific to Taiwan and southern Japan and sometimes in river estuaries. Barramundi are also farmed in the US in Massachusetts and in the UK in the New Forest. A similar fish called Nile perch is found in Lake Victoria, Africa.

Available Farmed fish available all year round. Wild fish available all year in northern Australia. Large fish sold as fillets and steaks. Farmed barramundi are usually smaller, weighing 450g–1.5kg (1–3lb) and sold whole.

Cooking Bake, grill, steam, fry, barbecue or use in fish soups. The favourite Aboriginal way of cooking is to wrap a whole fish in leaves from the wild ginger plant and bake in hot ashes.

Substitute Sea bass.

Tilefish
(alternative name golden bass)

Lopholatilus spp.

tile chameau (French), *blanquillo camello* (Spanish), *tile gibboso* (Italian), *blauer Ziegelfisch* (German), *peixe paleta camelo* (Portuguese), *amadai* (Japanese)

Emperor

Lethrinus spp.

capitaine (French), *Schnapper* (German), *bica* (Portuguese)

Characteristics As with sea bream, there are many different members of the emperor family including yellowtail/sky, snubnose, thumbprint, longface and spangled/blue emperors. Closely related to, and looking a lot like, snappers, they have slim bodies, sharp spines and can grow quite large, although most commercial fish tend to range from 400g (14oz) to 800g (1¾lb). Not as strong-tasting as snapper, the emperor's diet of shrimp and crabs still gives its flesh a good flavour.

Habitat Found in the tropical waters of the Pacific and Indian Oceans.

Available All year round. Whole fish and fillets.

Cooking Fry, grill, bake or steam. Whole fish can be baked in salt, but leave the scales on or the salt will draw out moisture and flavour from the flesh.

Substitute Snapper, bream.

Characteristics Sometimes called 'the clown of the sea' due its colourful appearance, six species of tilefish are caught along America's Atlantic coast. The most striking is the golden tilefish with its blue-green back fading to pearly white on the belly, red and blue marks, yellow-gold spots and deep blue shading around the eyes. Tilefish has firm, white, dense and meaty flesh that has been likened to lobster.

Habitat Only found in the United States, tilefish live in the Atlantic in a warm tunnel of water that runs along a narrow stretch of the ocean bed from Nova Scotia to Florida. Most prolific from Nantucket to Delaware Bay.

Available All year round. Small whole fish weighing upward of 2.25kg (5lb), or as thick fillets from larger fish.

Cooking Pan-fry, bake, poach, grill or eat raw as sashimi.

Substitute Amberjack, tilapia, grouper, snapper, shark.

Snapper

Lutjanus spp.

vivaneau (French), *pargo* (Spanish), *lutianido* (Italian), *Schnapper* (German), *luciano, goraz* (Portuguese),
maya-maya (Philippines), *pla kaphong* (Thai), *ikan merah* (Malaysian, Indonesia)

Related species: jobfish

Characteristics Over 200 varieties of snapper exist, including yellowtail, mangrove jack, goldband, silk, crimson and two-spot, but the undisputed star of the species is the red snapper. All have bulging eyes set high on their curved heads, but while most snappers weigh between 450g and 1kg (1–2¼lb), the big red can grow up to 14kg (31lb). The pale pink, flaky flesh with its attractive sweet taste is similar in most snappers and is usually served with its eye-catching skin on, which can be eaten, but be sure to scale the fish before cooking.

Habitat Deep-water fish found in all the world's warm seas. American red snapper and yellowtail are prime catches off the Florida coast.

Available All year round. Whole fish. Red snapper over 3kg (6½lb) sold as fillets and steaks.

Cooking Whole fish: pan-fry, grill, bake or steam. Fillets and supremes: pan-fry, grill or steam.

Substitute Emperor.

Moonfish
(alternative names opah, Hawaiian moonfish)

Mene spp.

chrysostome, lampris (French), *luna real, opa* (Spanish), *pesce re* (Italian), *Gotteslachs* (German),

peixe cravo (Portuguese), *akamanbo, mandai* (Japanese)

Characteristics Considered a good-luck fish in Hawaii, where, before local native species began to be promoted, fishermen would often give moonfish away rather than sell them. Straight out of a Disney cartoon, this colourful creature is round, with a thin body similar to pomfret, striking blue-green and pink skin, and brilliant red fins. Moonfish can weigh up to 100kg (220lb) and the rich, fatty, salmon-like flesh is suited to being cooked with other strong flavours. The flesh varies according to where it is on the fish: the loin being light orange and tender, the breast meat bright red and the cheek meat dark red and creamy-textured. Side flesh tends to be tougher and stringier.

Habitat Lives in the open ocean at depths of 90–365m (300–1200ft) in most warm waters and can swim as far as the UK in summer. Moonfish don't travel in shoals, so are not regularly available, but are often landed as bycatch by Pacific tuna boats.

Available All year round but most abundant from April to August. Sold as fillets.

Cooking Loin fillets are steak-like and can be grilled, pan-fried, seared like meat or eaten raw as sashimi. Other cuts need longer cooking to tenderise them.

Substitute Salmon, sea trout, tuna.

Croaker/Drum

(Species and alternative names include meagre, golden croaker, black-spot, soldier, whiskered/bearded, greyfin, tiger-toothed, spotted, Atlantic)

Micropogonias undulatus

Characteristics Around 275 small and medium-sized species belonging to the closely related croaker and drum families live around the world. Croakers make a unique 'croaking' sound caused by strong abdominal muscles that vibrate against the air bladder as they swim, while drums produce a 'drumming' sound when their heads poke above the water. A long dorsal fin stretches almost to the tail, and the large otoliths (flat, wavy 'stones') found in the ears and looking like ivory, are worn as jewellery or protective amulets. A low oil content means the flesh quickly dries out if overcooked.

Habitat Found in the estuaries of many major rivers worldwide, including Southeast Asia, the Atlantic and Pacific coasts of tropical South America, the Mediterranean and the Gulf of California, as well as the Atlantic coast of the US from Cape Cod to Mexico. A few species such as the reef croaker and spotted drum live in clear water among coral reefs but most prefer bays or riverbanks. Only one species – the freshwater drum – is a bottom-dwelling fish found in lakes and rivers, particularly the Mississippi. Fish farms are now being set up around the world to boost supplies.

Available Year round. Whole fish and fillets.

Cooking Fry, bake, smoke, grill, steam or 'blacken' Cajun-style.

Substitute Sea bass, sea bream.

Red mullet

Mullus barbatus, M. surmuletus

rouget barbet (French), *salmonete* (Spanish, Portuguese), *triglia* (Italian), *Meerbarbe* (German)

Characteristics A pretty fish, whose skin is an iridescent mix of orange, red-gold and rose pink. Of the two species caught, striped red mullet, with its sloping head and a yellow band running the length of its body, is considered the finest. Quite small – it could be mistaken for a slim goldfish – it ranges in size from 200g (7oz) to 1kg (2¼ pounds) but has a big flavour thanks to its diet of crustaceans. The delicate pale pink flesh works well with strong flavours like fennel, olives and fresh herbs, making it a popular choice in Mediterranean recipes, particularly those of Provence. A similar species called goatfish, found in Australia and the western Atlantic from New Jersey to Brazil, belongs to the same family.

Habitat Primarily a Mediterranean fish but also caught off the French Atlantic coast, in the Black Sea, off the coast of Florida and in UK waters.

Available All year round. Smaller fish sold whole; larger ones of 400–560g (14oz to 1¼lb) sold whole or as fillets.

Cooking Scale carefully because the skin is fine and delicate. Grill, fry, bake, steam or use in a fish stew.

Substitute Red snapper, goatfish.

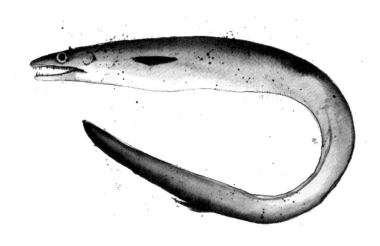

Conger pike
(alternative names dragon fish, daggertooth pike/conger)

Muraenesocidae

hamo (Japanese), *pla mangkor* (Thai), *malong* (Malaysian),
ca lat bac (Vietnamese), *moon sin* (Hong Kong)

Characteristics A type of eel measuring around 1.5m (5ft) in length with silvery skin that has a yellow or grey sheen. Its Thai name translates as dragon fish, a reference to its dagger-like array of teeth. It is highly regarded in Japanese cuisine, while the Chinese credit it with being both an aphrodisiac and a health-giving tonic when boiled with five-spice mix. Although good to eat, the white flesh is very bony, so is often used for making fish balls.

Habitat A marine eel found from India to Hong Kong that inhabits river estuaries and also migrates into fresh water.

Available All year round. Steaks.

Cooking Stews, soups, curries or fish balls.

Substitute Conger eel or other members of the eel family.

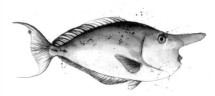

Soldier fish

Myripristis spp.

menpachi (Hawaii), *murjan* (India),
yogore-matsukasa (Japanese)

Characteristics
A medium-sized reef-dweller with a thin thin body and deep red and silvery skin marked with dark bands. Big-eyed and with a spiny dorsal fin, in Hawaii soldier fish is traditionally thought of as a guardian spirit. Closely related to the squirrel fish, it makes sounds like a squirrel's bark to warn intruders off its patch. Largely nocturnal, soldier fish remain hidden during the day in caves and crevasses feeding on plankton. Although the flesh has a good flavour, it is so bony that many fish lovers are put off eating it.

Habitat Soldier fish can be found in the tropical parts of the Atlantic and Pacific Oceans and from the Red Sea to the Philippines among rocky outcrops and reefs in shallow coastal waters.

Available All year round. Whole fish are generally about 15cm (6in) in length but can grow to twice that size.

Cooking Slash skin on both sides and pan-fry, barbecue or steam whole.

Substitute Snapper.

Unicorn fish

Naso spp.

kala lolo (Hawaii)

Characteristics
One look at this strange creature and the prominent horn between the eyes on its sloping forehead explains why it is named after the mythical unicorn. Related to the surgeonfish – its alternative name in Hawaii – it has a long oval body, skin as rough as sandpaper and two protruding spines near the tail that are said to be as sharp as a surgeon's scalpel. It feeds on algae, which flavour the mild white flesh, imparting the fragrance of whatever the fish has eaten, a favourite being limu lipoa seaweed in Hawaii.

Habitat Lives in clear tropical waters around coral reefs and rocky areas in the Andaman Sea, off the coast of northern Australia, in the Indian Ocean, waters of Southeast Asia and the Pacific around Hawaii and Japan. Over-fishing has severely depleted stocks in some areas, notably the Gulf of Siam.

Available All year round. Whole fish and fillets.

Cooking Grill, bake, poach or steam.

Substitute Grouper, jack/trevally, surgeonfish.

Sea bream
(alternative name porgy)

Pagellus bogaraveo, Sparus aurata, Spondyliosoma cantharus

Gilthead bream: *daurade royale* (French), *dorada* (Spanish), *orata* (Italian), *Goldbrassen* (German)

Red bream: *pageot rose* (French), *besugo* (Spanish), *pagro, pagello* (Italian), *nordischer Meerbrassen* (German), *goraz* (Portuguese)

Characteristics Gilthead and red are the best and most popular members of the 20-strong sea bream family, which are male for the first two years of their lives before undergoing a sex change and becoming female in their third year. Caught in the Mediterranean and off the Atlantic coast of Africa, other varieties include black (as above), black-banded, pink, white, dentex and Ray's bream. Most fish are small enough to serve whole and have firm, sweet, well-flavoured flesh.

Habitat Found over a huge area stretching from the Caribbean to the south coast of the UK and across the Atlantic from Cape Cod and Argentina to North Africa, sea bream are also farmed.

Available All year round when farmed. Wild black sea bream are in season from July to December, gilthead and red in the fall. Whole fish and fillets.

Cooking Small whole fish best cooked on the bone. Pan-fry, griddle, bake or steam whole fish and fillets.

Substitute Sea bass, emperor.

Coral trout

(alternative names leopard/passionfruit trout, leopard coral grouper)

Plectropomus spp.

lapo-lapo (Philippines), *suji-ara* (Japanese), *pla kaang daeng jutfa* (Thai), *tsut-sing-paan* (Hong Kong)

Related species: moon-tailed coral trout, footballer trout, blue-spot trout

Characteristics Growing to around 90cm (3ft) in length, this member of the grouper family can vary in colour from vivid pink to bright orange-red or brown and has small, brilliant blue spots over its head and body. Popular, particularly in the Far East, due to its good eating qualities and reasonable price, it has delicately flavoured flesh with fine white flakes.

Habitat Lives in open seas and around coral reefs in the Pacific from Japan to Australia, across Micronesia to Taiwan and Vietnam, and through the South China Sea to Thailand, Singapore, Malaysia and the Philippines.

Available All year round. Whole fish and fillets.

Cooking Bake, poach, grill or steam, but avoid too much handling as the flesh is delicate.

Substitute Sea bass, rascasse fillets, trout.

Moi

(alternatives names threadfish, Pacific threadfin, Hawaiian moi)

Polydactylus sexfilis

barbure (French), *barbudo seis barbas, pez barbita del Pacifico* (Spanish), *Fingerfisch* (German), *nanyo-agonashi, tsubamekonoshiro* (Japanese)

Characteristics This Hawaiian favourite is small, rounded and silvery with soft, flaky, rich flesh.

Habitat Over-fishing severely depleted stocks of wild fish by the 1990s. While numbers have been increased for sport fishing, moi for market are now farmed offshore in open-ocean submerged cages, the original fishponds having fallen into disuse through storm damage, silting up or becoming overgrown with mangroves.

Available Farmed fish all year round. Whole fish and fillets.

Cooking Despite a fairly high oil content, the flesh is easily overcooked, turning dry and rubbery, so it is often served rare or medium-rare. Steam or bake whole fish. Sear, pan-fry or grill fillets, with skin-side nearest the heat. Serve raw as sashimi.

Substitute Cod, haddock.

Threadfin

Polynemidae

Characteristics Over 33 species of threadfin are found in tropical and subtropical waters, ranging from the small black-finned variety, measuring around 20cm (8in), to the giant African threadfin that can grow to a whopping 2m (6½ft). Other species include Australia's king and blue varieties and the golden threadfin that is popular in Thailand. All species have long, elongated bodies, a large mouth, blunt nose and deeply forked tail. The flesh is white, moist and firm with a mild flavour and large flakes.

Habitat Feeds on small fish and crustaceans in open shallow coastal waters and rivers with muddy or sandy beds. Found from the west coast of India through Southeast Asia to Queensland, Australia.

Available All year round. Small species sold as whole fish. Larger ones as steaks, cutlets and fillets.

Cooking Whole fish: bake, barbecue, grill or fry. Steaks and cutlets: bake, grill, barbecue or fry. Fillets: bake, fry, grill, use in fish stews and fishcakes.

Substitute Bream, perch, morwong, barramundi.

Parrotfish

Scarus spp.

perroquet (French), *vieja* (Spanish), *pesci pappagallo* (Italian), *Papageifisch, Seepapagei* (German), *papagaiao* (Portuguese)

Characteristics Around 100 species of parrotfish swim the world's tropical seas, the most recognizable being the stoplight parrotfish (above) and the blue-barred parrotfish with its bright yellow skin and shimmering turquoise spots. Named for its parrot-like beak, which has numerous teeth for nibbling algae and soft-bodied reef-dwellers and is strong enough to crunch the hardest coral into fine sand. Hump-backed with a long, low dorsal fin, it has firm flesh with a mild flavour.

Habitat A reef fish with a very wide territory stretching from South and East Africa, to Australia and the Gulf of California.

Available All year round. Most fish weigh between 680g (1½lb) and 1kg (2¼lb).

Cooking Bake, fry, steam or grill smaller fish on the bone. Larger fish can be filleted and cooked in the same way. Strong flavours such as chilli, Thai spices and coconut go well with it.

Substitute Wrasse, snapper.

Rabbit fish
(alternative name spinefoot)

Siganus spp.

beronang lada (India), samaral (Philippines), pla salit (Thai), dengkis (Malaysian), nai maan (Hong Kong)

Characteristics Closely related to surgeonfish, the rabbit fish has a similar flat, thin, oval body but also sharp dorsal spines that can inflict a painful cut. With around 30 species, skin colour can vary, but one of the most common is dark olive peppered with hundreds of small pearly dots on the upper side. The fish gets its name from its small, slightly protruding mouth, large dark eyes and rabbit-like habit of constantly munching the algae it feeds on. The white flesh is firm and good to eat.

Habitat Found from the Arabian Gulf through the warm waters of Southeast Asia to southern China

and Australia, where it is believed to be helping protect the Great Barrier Reef by keeping the levels of algae down.

Available All year round. Whole fish and fillets.

Cooking Pan-fry, grill and steam. Whole fish can also be barbecued and are popular at Chinese New Year when they are said to be particularly good.

Substitute Grouper, soldierfish, jack/trevally.

Barracuda
(alternative name giant sea pike)

Sphyraena spp.

brochet de mer, barracouda (French), *barracuda, espeton, espet* (Spanish), *luccio marino, barracuda* (Italian), *Pfeilhecht, Barracuda* (German), *bicuda* (Portuguese)

Characteristics Long and thin with a forked tail and razor-sharp teeth, the barracuda looks fearsome but the sweet-tasting, flaky, pink-fawn flesh is buttery, delicious and melts in the mouth. Two of the main species are the great barracuda, which has black spots on the underside, and the yellowtail, which has no dark marks but does have a yellow tail. Strong, spicy Thai, Indian and Cajun flavours complement its rich-tasting flesh well and the skin crisps beautifully when grilled or fried.

Habitat Found in warm waters worldwide, including the Pacific (where around 20 different species live),

the Caribbean, the western Atlantic, Indian Ocean, the Arabian Gulf and the Red Sea.

Available All year round but seasonal in different areas. Small whole fish (weighing less than 2kg/4½lb), long fillets and supremes from larger fish (up to 8kg/18 pounds).

Cooking Pan-fry, grill, bake.

Substitute Kingfish.

Pompano

Trachinotus spp.

palometa (Spanish), *leccia stella* (Italian), *Gabelmakrele* (German), *kobanaji* (Japanese)

Characteristics Firm, rich-flavoured flesh makes the pompano one of the finest-tasting fish there is and it is particularly prized in the US where the superior American, Atlantic and Florida varieties are all harvested. A member of the jack family, its deep, flattened body has silvery skin, fatty flesh, a small mouth and a forked tail. Around 20 different types are landed around the world and are of varying quality. They include the African pompano, snubnose pompano and a Latin American species of palometa, common in south Florida and South America, that is thinner, coarser and more oily.

Habitat Off the Gulf coast of Florida, the Caribbean and in the Indian and Pacific Oceans where they live among the coral reefs feeding off smaller fish.

Available All year round, the peak season in the US being spring to fall. Usually sold whole and either fresh or frozen, weighing around 900g (2lb). If they have not previously been frozen, they freeze well.

Cooking Score flesh on both sides and fry, bake, grill or steam.

Substitute Bream, snapper.

Pout
(alternative name pouting)

Trisopterus luscus

tacaud (French), *faneca* (Spanish, Portuguese), *merluzzo francese* (Italian), *Franzosendorsch* (German)

Characteristics A small member of the cod family that grows to 30cm (12in) or less. Its fragile white flesh has a mild, pleasant flavour but needs careful handling as it can easily spoil. It is best eaten as fresh as possible as it also deteriorates quickly. Pout has the same three dorsal fins and two central fins as other cod family members, a body that tapers towards the tail and a large barbel jutting out of the lower jaw. A curious membrane covers the eyes – explaining the original name of 'bib' or 'bien', an old word for blister.

Habitat Found in shallow water within a few yards of the shore from northern Europe to southern Spain. In warmer climates larger fish move out to deeper, cooler water during the hot summer months.

Available All year round. Whole fish and fillets.

Cooking Fry, bake, grill, steam or poach.

Substitute Pollock, cod, whiting.

Herring

Clupea spp.

hareng (French), *arenque* (Spanish, Portuguese), *aringa* (Italian), *Hering* (German), *sild* (Norwegian, Danish, Icelandic)

Characteristics A smooth, slender-bodied fish with scales that can easily be rubbed off with the fingers. The skin is dark blue along the back, shading to silvery white below, with hints of green and gold. Herring usually range in size from 100g (4oz) to 450g (1lb) and have off-white fatty flesh that is soft and unctuous. Swimming in immense shoals, they make a strange squeaking noise when netted, thought to be caused by air being expelled from their air bladder.

Habitat An important fish in northern Europe but found right across the cold northern waters of the Atlantic as far south as Chesapeake Bay in the west and northern France in the east. A related species is also caught in the Pacific. Over-fishing and fluctuating stocks have seen the rapid decline of the herring industry in many countries.

Available Season varies depending on where caught but mostly at their best in spring and summer. Whole fish sold fresh but herring is also popular in various smoked, pickled and cured forms (see page 203).

Cooking Grill or bake and serve with a sharp sauce such as mustard. A traditional Scottish recipe is to roll herring in oats and fry in bacon fat. Soft (fresh) herring roes on toast are considered a delicacy.

Substitute Large sardines, mackerel.

Whitebait

Clupea spp.

poutine (French), *aladroch* (Spanish), *bianchetti* (Italian)

Characteristics Not a species in its own right but the inch-long fry of small, silvery fish, typically herring, sprat, sardine or anchovy in Europe, silverside or sand-eel in the US, and inanga in New Zealand. Whitebait are sweet and succulent. In the early 17th century small fry swarmed the River Thames and London taverns began promoting special whitebait feasts. They became particularly popular during the 19th century when a gathering for the British prime minister and his cabinet, revolving around the consumption of these tiny, translucent fish, became an annual event.

Habitat Fished in estuaries, shallow coastal waters, the North Sea, and the east Atlantic.

Available Usually frozen in bags. Whole fish.

Cooking Dust whole fish in seasoned flour and deep-fry. Cayenne or chilli powder can be added to the flour for a spicy kick.

Substitute Small fry of locally caught oily fish.

Saury

(alternative names needlefish, skipper)

Cololabis spp., Scomberesox spp.

aiguille de mer, balaou (French), *paparda* (Spanish), *costardello, gastaurello* (Italian), *Makrelenheckte* (German), *agulhao* (Portuguese)

Characteristics Long and thin, saury can grow to almost 50cm (20in) in length. Small, weighing only 85–170g (3–6oz) each, saury have finlets near the tail, a long beak, and full-flavoured, firm flesh.

Habitat Caught on both sides of the Atlantic, the Mediterranean and off the coast of Australia. Normally found in the warm seas around the latitude of Madeira, in the summer months saury migrate north as far as Norway, Iceland and Newfoundland.

In North America fishermen employ the Japanese method of using lights to draw the fish towards their boats, then scooping them up in nets. A related species, called the Pacific saury or mackerel pike, is fished from Japan to the Gulf of Alaska and south to Mexico.

Available Atlantic saury, all year round. Pacific saury, autumn and winter. Whole fish.

Cooking Pan-fry, poach or braise in a sauce.

Anchovy

Engraulis spp.

anchois (French), *boqueron* (Spanish), *acciuga, alice* (Italian), *Sardelle* (German), *biqueirao* (Portuguese)

Characteristics A small silvery fish, only 7.5–10cm (3–4in) long, with a rich, mildly oily flavour and off-white, soft-textured flesh. It swims in vast shoals and much of the European anchovy catch goes for processing to canning factories. A related species, caught in the Pacific off the west coast of the US, has a shark-like mouth and long nose. Again, many go to be processed, but eaten fresh they have a stronger, oilier flavour than European anchovies.

Habitat Fished in deep waters around Spain and Portugal all the way up the Atlantic coast to Brittany, throughout the Mediterranean and in the Black Sea. The Pacific anchovy is found from British Columbia to Baja California.

Available At their best in the spring from April to June. Whole fish and butterfly fillets.

Cooking Grill, barbecue, pan-fry, bake or hot-smoke.

Substitute Small sardines.

Tuna

Katsuwonus pelamis, Thunnus spp.

thon (French), *atun* (Spanish), *tonno* (Italian), *Thun* (German), *atum* (Portuguese), *kuromaguro (bluefin)* (Japanese)

Species: bluefin/tunny, bigeye, albacore/long fin, skipjack, yellowfin

Characteristics With its firm, full-flavoured flesh, a tuna steak is the marine equivalent of the finest beef tenderloin. Tuna flesh varies in colour according to the species: bluefin, the largest and most expensive, has bright red flesh and is considered the finest for sashimi and sushi, although over-fishing has seriously endangered stocks. Albacore is smaller with creamy pink flesh and is most often canned as 'white meat', while the closely related bigeye and yellowfin varieties have browner flesh and are best eaten cooked. Skipjack, making up half the world's catch, has light flesh and is almost exclusively sold canned, although darker-fleshed skipjack are used for sashimi in Japan.

Habitat These monarchs of the ocean migrate in large shoals through the warmer seas of the globe, living from the Mediterranean to the Gulf of Mexico, across the Pacific, and through the waters of Southeast Asia.

Available All year round but can be harder to source in the summer when fish follow the monsoon season around the Pacific. Steaks.

Cooking Pan-fry, grill, barbecue or serve raw as sushi and sashimi. Avoid baking as the flesh will dry out. Tuna is best when seared on the outside and left rare in the centre so that it retains its moist texture and flavour. Asian and Mediterranean flavourings work well but creamy sauces are best avoided.

Substitute Marlin, swordfish.

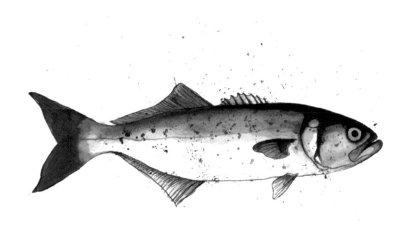

Bluefish

Pomatomus saltatrix

coupe fil, tassergal (French), *anchoa de bando, anjova, chova* (Spanish), *pesce serra* (Italian), *Blaufisch, Tassergal* (German),
anchova, tasergal (Portuguese), *amikiri, okisuzuki* (Japanese), *tailor* (Australia), *scad* (South Africa)

Characteristics A great sport fish, bluefish needs to be eaten as soon as possible after landing because its flesh deteriorates quickly. A well-proportioned fish with pale grey-blue skin, it has a voracious appetite for smaller sardine-like fish and is extremely predatory – once landed it's best to stay clear of its fiercely snapping jaws! The larger the fish, the stronger and richer the flavour, the greyish white flesh becoming lighter when cooked.

Habitat Caught throughout the Mediterranean, especially around Tunisia and Turkey, and in the western Atlantic. On the east coast of the US,

bluefish are found from Florida to Maine and related species are popular game fish in Australia and South Africa.

Available All year round, although most abundant in late summer. Some areas have local restrictions during spawning seasons. Whole fish weighing from 2.25kg (5lb) upwards and fillets.

Cooking Pan-fry, grill, bake or hot-smoke.

Substitute Mackerel, bonito, herring.

Bonito

Sarda spp.

bonet à dos raye (French), *bonit atlantico, sarda* (Spanish), *palamita* (Italian), *Pelamide* (German), *sarrajao* (Portuguese)

Characteristics This member of the mackerel family looks and tastes halfway between mackerel and tuna. Ranging in size from 1–5kg (2¼–11lb), the pale pink flesh is more coarsely textured and drier than tuna with quite a strong taste. Fast swimmers, bonito often leap out of the water when feeding.

Habitat Atlantic bonito is fished as far north as Cape Cod in the west and the south of Britain in the east. Two related species are found off the Pacific coasts of North and South America: the Pacific bonito and the striped bonito. Others are the frigate mackerel/bullet tuna, caught in tropical waters, and kawakawa from the west Pacific.

Available Summer (and fall in the Pacific).

Cooking Bake, grill, pan-fry, barbecue, casserole or smoke. Remove skin after cooking. Dried bonito flakes are used to make Japanese fish stock.

Substitute Tuna, mackerel.

Sardine/Pilchard

Sardinus pilchardus

sardine (French), *sardina* (Spanish, Italian), *Pilchard, Sardine* (German), *sardinha* (Portuguese)

Characteristics Small, metallic-silver fish with a greenish back and pointed head. Sardines range in size from 85–140g (3–5oz), the larger, older fish being known as pilchards. Sardines' soft, dark, fatty flesh makes them particularly suited to grilling and their skin, once scaled, crisps beautifully.

Habitat Fished off the south coast of the UK, the French Atlantic coast and in the Mediterranean, sardines live in shoals. Related species include the sardinella, which is found in the Indian and Pacific Oceans and throughout Southeast Asia. Over-fishing along the Pacific coast of the US, particularly around Monterey's Cannery Row, led to sardines virtually disappearing there after the 1930s, but today stocks are gradually being built back up.

Available Europe: May to October. Availability elsewhere varies, but most common in summer. Whole fish.

Cooking Grill.

Mackerel

Scomber scombrus

maquereau, lisette (small fish) (French), *caballa* (Spanish), *maccarello, sgombro* (Italian),
Makrele (German), *sarda* (Portuguese)

Characteristics One of the richest sources of omega-3, mackerel has a slim, silvery blue, bullet shaped body with dark wavy stripes on its back. The greyish-fawn flesh has a rich, oily flavour and must be eaten very fresh – so much so that at Billingsgate fish market in 17th-century London traders could sell mackerel on Sundays when all other trade was forbidden.

Habitat Atlantic mackerel travel in large shoals from the Mediterranean to the icy waters of Norway, Iceland, and Labrador. Related species include king mackerel, found in subtropical seas from North Carolina to Brazil and the Arabian Gulf to Japan, Indian/chub mackerel, fished from the Indian ocean to the Pacific, and Spanish mackerel, from Cape Cod to Mexico and across the Pacific.

Available All year round but best in spring/autumn. Whole fish, fillets. Fresh and smoked.

Cooking Pan-fry, grill or bake, and serve with a sharp sauce such as gooseberry or cranberry. Use in fish pâtés and curries.

Substitute Large sardines, herring.

Sprat

Sprattus sprattus

esprot (French), *espadin* (Spanish), *papalina* (Italian), *Sprotte, Sprot, Breitling* (German),
espadilha (Portuguese)

Characteristics Herring's little brother, a sprat grows to a maximum length of only 14cm (5½in). Having a deep bluish green back and silvery belly and sides, the belly is deeply curved with spiny scales running from the throat to the vent in front of its anal fin. The flesh is similar to the herring's, creamy white with a soft, fatty but delicate flavour.

Habitat Once fished in large numbers in the River Thames, sprats are now found seasonally around the UK, in the western Atlantic and from the north of Norway to the Mediterranean. In the Baltic, a related species is an important catch. Southeast Asia's dark green-gold and silver rainbow sardine, sold both fresh and dried, is similar and has tasty, flaky flesh.

Available Autumn, winter, spring. Whole fish. Fresh, smoked, cured (see page 195).

Cooking Grill, barbecue, griddle or pan-fry.

Substitute Herring, sardine, anchovy, rainbow sardine.

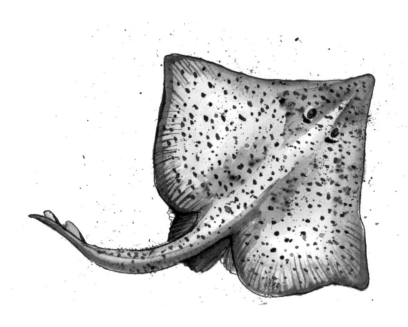

Skate

Dipturus batis

raie, pocheteau (French), *noriega* (Spanish), *moro* (Italian), *Glattroche* (German), *raia* (Portuguese)

Characteristics The same family as ray and looking similar, skate is distinguishable by its long snout. Growing to a length of about 2m (6½ft), it has a grey or brown back dotted with light and black spots and a spotted blue-grey or ash-coloured underside. When cooked, the sweet white flesh slides easily off the cartilaginous ribs that run through its wings.

Habitat Skate lives on the seabed and is caught from the Mediterranean to Iceland and the north of Norway. A related species, the barndoor skate, is found in North American waters.

Available All year round. Sold as wing portions.

Cooking Deep-fry, pan-fry, poach, steam or bake.

Substitute Any species of ray.

Mako shark
(alternative name bonito shark)

Isurus oxyrinchus

mako, taupe bleu (French), *marrajo* (Spanish), *squalo mako, ossirina* (Italian), *Mako, Makrelenhai* (German), *tuberao-anequim* (Portuguese)

Characteristics Sleek and beautiful, with a sharp nose and metallic-blue back shading to white below, in the US the mako is considered one of the best eating sharks. A fast swimmer, it can leap up to 6m (20ft) out of the water and fights ferociously when caught, making it a challenging sport fish. The white flesh has a full-bodied flavour and is similar to swordfish, although less dry.

Habitat Caught in subtropical and warm temperate waters in the north and south Atlantic, as well as in the Mediterranean, Caribbean and Gulf of Mexico.

Available All year round. Sold as steaks.

Cooking Grill, pan-fry, deep-fry, barbecue, use for soups, stews, and kebabs and in Cajun 'blackened' recipes.

Substitute Other species of shark, swordfish.

Porbeagle shark

Lamna nasus

taupe (French), *cailon, marrajo* (Spanish), *smeriglio* (Italian), *Heringshai* (German), *tuberao-sardo* (Portuguese)

Characteristics Another popular species of shark from the hundreds that swim the world's oceans. A porbeagle can grow 3–4m (10–13ft) in length, its body is bluish-grey above and white below, and despite its ferocious-looking teeth it tends to be docile when hooked, in contrast to the aggressive mako. Its fairly coarse flesh is white, has a good flavour and, as with the mako, is similar to swordfish. Other commonly eaten species of shark include tope, blackfin and hammerhead.

Habitat Found on both sides of the Atlantic – from the Mediterranean to the southwest coast of the UK and the cool waters between Orkney and Iceland, and from the Carolinas to Newfoundland.

Available All year round. Sold as steaks.

Cooking Grill, pan-fry, deep-fry, grill, use for soups, stews and kebabs, and in Cajun 'blackened' recipes.

Substitute Other species of shark, swordfish.

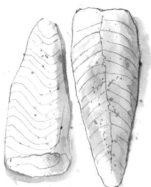

Monkfish
(alternative names angler fish, goosefish)

Lophius spp.

lotte, baudroie (French), *rape* (Spanish), *rospo, rana pescatrice* (Italian), *Angler, Seeteufel* (German),
tamboril (Portuguese)

Characteristics The ugly sister of the marine world with a huge gaping mouth and trailing 'fishing lines' on its head – hence its alternative name of 'angler'. This aggressive carnivore was originally used for scampi, a cheap alternative to Dublin bay prawns, but is now highly prized in its own right. The bright white flesh is dense, lobster-like, and holds its shape when cooked.

Habitat Both deep water and inshore, these bottom-dwelling fish are caught throughout the Mediterranean and around the Iberian peninsula to the British Isles. Over 150 species exist worldwide including stargazers in Australia and New Zealand, which are similar but have bones rather than cartilage. In the US monkfish stocks are severely depleted and the fish is on the endangered list.

Available All year round. As the head accounts for well over half the total body weight, usually only the skinned tail is sold, although the head is good for making stock.

Cooking Peel off the fine grey membrane covering the flesh. Grill, bake, roast, pan-fry or barbecue as kebabs. The liver is also extremely good and is much appreciated in Japan as sashimi and in the US, where, before stocks of monkfish became so low, chefs served it as a marine version of foie gras.

Substitute No real alternative; langoustine meat is closest.

Skate

Raja brachyura

raie lisse (French), *raya boca de rosa* (Spanish),
razza (Italian), *Keulen-stachel* (German),
raia-pontuada (Portuguese)

Characteristics Many species of ray are caught worldwide including the shovelnosed, roker/thornback and Cambodian spotted eagle rays. In the US all rays are called skate. Most have brownish grey skin, the colour varying according to habitat. Adult fish, weighing 6.8–11.3kg (15–25lb), have prickles covering their backs, while younger fish have smooth skin. The wing flesh is white, flaky and well flavoured.

Habitat A bottom-dweller that rests camouflaged on the seabed waiting for its next meal to drift by. Blonde ray are caught off the west and southern coasts of England and the northwestern coast of Scotland.

Available Blonde ray available most of the year. Other species dependent on where caught. Wing portions.

Cooking Best eaten several days after being caught. Pan-fry, deep-fry, bake or poach.

Substitute Other species of ray, plaice.

Dogfish

(alternative names spiny dogfish shark, huss, rock salmon, rock eel, Cape shark)

Schyliorhinus spp.

petite roussette, saumonette (French), *pintarroja* (Spanish),
spinarola, gattopardo (Italian),
Katzenhai (German), *pata-roxa* (Portuguese)

Characteristics A junior member of the shark family that can grow to 75cm (2½ft), with strong jaws and sharp teeth for crushing small fish and crustaceans. Several species exist, the most common in Europe being the lesser spotted, which has very abrasive brown or sandy-coloured skin speckled with tiny dark spots. The white flesh has a sweet, mild flavour and is flaky but firm. A high oil content stops it drying out when cooked.

Habitat Lesser spotted dogfish are caught mainly in the north Atlantic. Other, larger, species are fished in the US, Canada, New Zealand and Chile as well as European waters.

Available All year round. Sold as skinned steaks or fillets.

Cooking Deep-fry in batter, pan-fry or bake.

Substitute Cod, hake, haddock.

Wahoo
(alternative names jack mackerel, Pacific king-fish, queen fish)

Acanthocybium solandri

paere, thazard bâtard (French), *sierra, peto* (Spanish), *acantocibio, maccerello striato* (Italian),
Peto (German), *cavala da India* (Portuguese), *kamasu-sawara* (Japanese), *ono* (Hawaii)

Characteristics A near relative of the king mackerel, wahoo is a prime eating fish. The flesh is a pale, translucent pink when raw but cooks up white and firm and has a mild, almost chicken-like flavour and texture. The body is marked with vertical bands of wavy electric blue lines, the underbelly is silver, and the long lower jaw has razor-sharp teeth.

Habitat Solitary fish that are highly prized as game, wahoo are found worldwide in tropical and sub-tropical seas from Australia and Fiji to Hawaii, South America and the Caribbean. In Florida they are frequently a bycatch of tuna and swordfish.

Available All year round, although more prolific in summer. Fillets and thick steaks.

Cooking Pan-fry, grill or hot-smoke. A piquant marinade spiked with chilli and lime juice adds flavour and helps keep the flesh moist.

Substitute Mahi mahi, kingfish, mackerel, tuna.

Jack/trevally

Carangidae

Characteristics Jack and trevally are the commercial names for a wide range of interrelated species of fish distributed throughout the warmer waters of the world. With silver skins and dense full-flavoured white flesh, they are known by various local names, the most common including crevalle jack, bigeye trevally, orange-spotted trevally, African pompano and yellowtail kingfish; the latter not to be confused with a true Kingfish (see page 101).

Habitat Coral-reef dwellers, where they tend to gather in shoals to feed off smaller reef fish. The Australian yellowtail kingfish is now being successfully farmed, producing a regular supply of 4–8kg (9–18lb) fish.

Available All year round. Fillets. A relative of the yellowtail from New Zealand is the King George trevally, which has deliciously delicate flesh and is available whole or as fillets.

Cooking Pan-fry, bake or grill. Citrus marinades help retain the moisture in the flesh during cooking and strong Thai and Cajun flavours work well with it too.

Substitute Black cod, tilapia, pompano.

Snook

(alternative names sergeant fish,
ravallia, salt water pike)

Centropomus spp.

crossie-blanc (French), *snoek* (Dutch), *bicudo* (Portuguese),
brochet de mer (Cuba, French),
robalo (Latin America)

Characteristics The
snook is an immensely
powerful fish and
puts up a terrific fight
when hooked. Its soft
blue-grey colouring is
unremarkable except
for a black lateral
line running down its
length. The flesh is firm,
moderately oily and has
an excellent flavour.
Snook can weigh up to
23kg (50lb) but average
nearer 2.25–3.5kg
(5–8lb).

Habitat Native to
the western Atlantic
from Florida to Rio de

Janeiro, snook live in
shallow coastal waters,
estuaries and lagoons,
sometimes entering fresh
water. Caught both for
sport and the table in
Latin America and the
Caribbean, snook are
not sold commercially in
the US.

Available All year
round. Whole fish
and fillets.

Cooking Grill, pan-fry,
steam, hot-smoke, bake
or use in fish stews and
soups. The bitter skin is
not eaten.

Morwong

(alternative name rubberlip morwong)

Cheilodactylidae spp.

Characteristics The
Mick Jagger of the fish
world, it's not hard to
see how the morwong
got its alternative name
of rubberlip. Growing
to around 45cm (2½ft)
and 6kg (13½lb),
several species are
fished including blue,
red-banded and jackass
morwongs, the quality
of their mild, medium to
firm, pale pink/creamy
flesh being dependent on
what they eat. As well as
protruding lips, morwong
have horn-like bumps in
front of the eyes and a
frilly forked tail.

Habitat A popular sport
fish living in the waters
of the continental shelf

around southeastern
and Western Australia
and off the North Island
of New Zealand, where
restrictions on minimum
size apply. Also found in
the Pacific from Japan
and China to Hawaii,
where they search for
food on the ocean floor.

Available All year
round. Whole fish
and fillets.

Cooking Grill, pan-fry
or wrap in foil or banana
leaves with Thai spices
and coconut and bake.

Substitute Bream,
snapper.

Giant hawkfish
(alternative name Chinese grouper)

Cirrhitidae

épervier géant (French), *chino mero* (Spanish)

Characteristics This largest member of the hawkfish family can weigh up to 4kg (9lb) and has the unique ability to perch on its pectoral fin. Its deep, compressed body has mainly olive skin that is marked with irregular golden vertical bars said to resemble Chinese patterns, hence its alternative name. The firm, white flesh has large flakes and an excellent flavour.

Habitat A solitary fish that lives in shallow waters around large rock formations of offshore islands. Caught off both the east and west coasts of Africa, in the Indian and Atlantic Oceans, and in the eastern Pacific from the Gulf of California to northern Colombia and west to the Galapagos Islands.

Available All year round depending on where caught. Fillets.

Cooking Pan-fry, grill, deep-fry and use in chowders and fish stews.

Substitute Other members of the hawkfish and grouper families.

Conger eel

Conger conger

congre (French), *congrio* (Spanish), *grongo* (Italian), *Congeraal, Meeraal, Conger* (German), *congro* (Portuguese)

Characteristics Large, with a pointed head, sharp teeth and a fat serpentine body that can grow up to 3m (10ft) in length. Its grey-white flesh is firm and has a good flavour but is also bony, so middle cuts of large fish are best.

Habitat Conger eels range from the Mediterranean to the southwest coast of Britain, decreasing in numbers as the sea cools towards Norway and Iceland. Lurking in wrecks and rocky crevices by day, these solitary swimmers come out at night to feed on fish, crustaceans and even octopus, their principal enemy.

Available All year round. Steaks.

Cooking Middle, less bony cuts, can be roasted or baked and served with a well-flavoured sauce. Use the meat from the bony tail end in fish pies and soups and the head and bones for stock.

Substitute Cod, haddock and other firm white fish.

Mahi mahi

(alternative name dolphin fish)

Coryphaena hippurus

coryphene commune (French), *lampuga, dorado* (Spanish), *lampuga, contaluzzo* (Italian), *Goldmakrele* (German), *dorado* (Portuguese), *lampuka* (Maltese)

Characteristics Now known by its Hawaiian name, mahi mahi (which translates as 'strong-strong') are in fact unrelated to dolphins. A solitary fish with a long, slender, silvery body covered in an iridescent array of black, gold and blue spots, it has firm pink flesh that is delicately flavoured.

Habitat Widely distributed around the globe in warmer waters, particularly the south Atlantic, Caribbean, Gulf of Mexico, Hawaii, the Seychelles and the south Pacific. Mahi mahi is also caught in Malta during late summer, and is known as lampuka.

Available Season runs from spring to fall with regional variations. Usually sold as fillets. Frozen is available, but it is best when fresh.

Cooking Grill, bake, pan-fry, hot-smoke or use in 'blackened' Cajun recipes.

Substitute Tuna, mackerel.

Sailfish

Istiophorus spp.

voilier (French), *pez vela* (Spanish), *pesce vela* (Italian), *Segelfisch* (German), *veleiro* (Portuguese)

Characteristics Like the marlin, this warm-water fish can grow to an enormous size and speeds though the sea like a torpedo. It has the same long, pointed snout as the marlin, plus a jutting lower jaw, blue-grey back and sides, and a white belly. 'Sail' comes from the spectacular, deep sapphire blue dorsal fin, which folds neatly away while the fish swims but unwraps to its full glory if it feels under threat or to round up shoals of smaller fish for dinner. The flesh is solid and meaty like that of marlin and can be fairly tough.

Habitat Two species are found in warm and temperate waters: the Atlantic and the Indo-Pacific sailfish. Both swim near the ocean surface and are popular game fish rather than commercial fish.

Available Usually all year round but may be seasonal according to where caught. Steaks or fillets.

Cooking Grill, pan-fry, or sear on a griddle.

Substitute Marlin, swordfish, tuna.

Escolar

(alternative names white tuna, snake mackerel)

Lepidocybium flavobrunneum

escolier (French), *escolar negro, sierna* (Spanish), *tirsite* (Italian), *foguete, senuca* (Portuguese), *Snoek* (UK and German), *walu* (Hawaii and Fiji), *barakuta* (Japanese)

Characteristics Growing up to 2m (6½ft) in length, the escolar has a large mouth, tiny finlets and dark brown skin that darkens to almost black as it ages. The creamy white flesh turns snow white when cooked, is oil-rich and strongly flavoured.

Habitat Lives in tropical and temperate waters around the world. Fished in the Pacific, particularly around Fiji, Hawaii, and Australia, the Gulf of Mexico, and Indonesia.

Available Late winter through spring. Sold as fillets. A related species, sometimes called escolar, but actually oilfish or castor oil fish, should be avoided as its reddish flesh contains so much oil that it acts as a laxative.

Cooking Grill, pan-sear, bake, steam or eat raw as sushi and sashimi. Skin before eating.

Substitute Orange roughy, icefish, black cod.

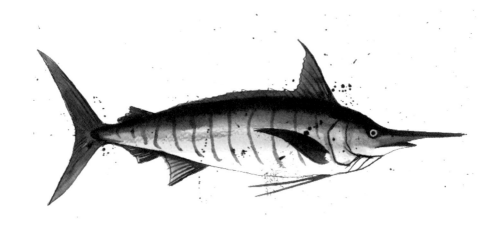

Marlin

Makaira spp.

makaire (French), *marlin, pez aguda* (Spanish), *pesce lancia* (Italian), *Marlin, Speerfisch* (German),
espadim (Portuguese), *kajiki* (Japanese)

Characteristics A member of the billfish family that can grow very large indeed. It can reach 2.4m (8ft) long and weigh 450kg (1,000lb), although 22kg (50lb) is an average size. An incredibly fast swimmer, marlin is capable of reaching speeds of nearly 112kmh (70mph). It has a long spear-like snout similar to swordfish, but less fatty flesh. The slender body has smooth, shiny skin with a long, rigid dorsal fin that peaks crest-like on its back. The dense pale pink meaty flesh is a source of omega-3 fatty acids.

Habitat Fished worldwide in warm and temperate waters. The blue marlin is widely distributed through the earth's tropical seas and is prized as a sport fish, black marlin and the huge striped marlin are found in the Pacific and Indian Oceans, and white marlin in the Caribbean and western Mediterranean.

Available All year round, although seasons may vary according to where caught. Skin-on boneless steaks.

Cooking Cook on a griddle, pan-fry, braise, bake, grill and hot-smoke.

Substitute Tuna, swordfish, sailfish.

Kingfish
(alternative name king mackerel)

Menticirrhus spp., Scomberomorus spp.

thazard serra (French), *sierra* (Spanish), *scombro reale* (Italian), *Konigsmakrele* (German), *serra* (Portuguese)

Characteristics With robust, oily flesh that holds together well, this big brother of the mackerel needs to be cooked with piquant spicy or citrus flavours to be enjoyed at its best. A long, slender fish with small fins and a pointed snout, it has a dark grey back that shades to silver below. The whole of the body is covered with very small, barely visible scales.

Habitat A fast swimmer found in warm waters from the Red Sea and Arabian Gulf through the Indian

Ocean and down the Atlantic coasts of North and South America from North Carolina to Rio de Janeiro.

Available All year round. Fillets and steaks.

Cooking Grill, pan-fry or bake. It is important not to overcook fillets or they will dry out.

Substitute Tuna, mackerel.

Moray eel

Muraenidae

Characteristics Although there are more than 100 varieties of moray eel, the conger eel's more decorative cousin, only a few are fished commercially and some are known to cause ciguatera fish poisoning (see page 13). A moray can grow to around 1.5m (5ft) and has a large head, wide jaws and a vividly patterned body that acts as camouflage. It relies on a highly developed sense of smell to sniff out its prey of other fish and crustaceans, which it tears apart with its sharp teeth. As with conger eel, the soft, white flesh can be bony and is extremely difficult to skin.

Habitat A shy, solitary creature, it hides in crevices in coral reefs close to its prey in sub-tropical and temperate waters. It is widely fished in the Indian Ocean, the western Atlantic around Bermuda, Southeast Asia, Fiji and Australia.

Available All year round. Steaks.

Cooking Deep-fry, roast, bake and use in fish soups such as bouillabaisse.

Substitute Conger eel, cod.

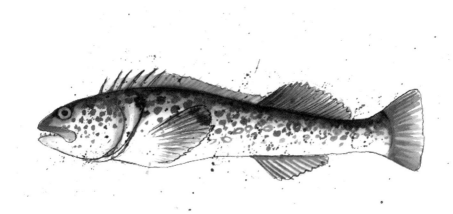

Lingcod
(alternative names blue, buffalo, green or white cod)

Ophiodon elongatus

terpuga buffalo (French), *bacalao largo, lorcha* (Spanish), *ofiodonte* (Italian),
langer Grunling (German), *lorcha* (Portuguese), *ainame* (Japanese)

Characteristics A member of the greenling family of fish rather than a true cod or ling. This fearsome creature with its giant mouth is an extremely aggressive opponent when hooked so is highly rated by adventurous anglers. The dull brown-grey skin is spotted in various smoky shades, and the dense, meaty flesh, which has a blue-green hue when raw but turns brilliant white when cooked, is moist with large, soft flakes.

Habitat A marine fish unique to the northeast Pacific from the Gulf of Alaska to Baja California but most abundant off the coast of British Columbia. Found on the sea bottom around rocky crevices

or ledges, lingcod range from 1.3–9kg (3–20lb), although monsters of 36kg (80lb) are not unknown.

Available Peak season is April to August. Over-fishing has led to Alaska enforcing a strictly limited season that starts later on July 1. Whole fish, steaks and fillets.

Cooking Popular in the northwest states of the US as upmarket fish and chips. It can also be baked, pan-fried or grilled. Northwest coastal native Americans grill lingcod on a cedar plank with delicious results.

Substitute Cod, haddock, hoki, hake.

Cobia
*(alternative names black kingfish,
black salmon, lemonfish, crabeater, runner,
sergeant fish)*

Rachycentron canadum

*mafou (French), Offizierfisch (German), fogueteiro galego
(Portuguese), dagat dagat (Philippines), sugi (Japanese),
pla chawn thaleh (Thai)*

Characteristics The only game fish belonging to the mackerel family, cobia has a long, slender body, a flattened head, and can grow up to 45cm (2½ft) in length. The skin is smooth with small scales and brown on the back shading to white on the belly with two darker brown horizontal bands. The white flesh is firm with an excellent flavour.

Habitat Living around reefs, rocky outcrops and harbours, cobia is caught in warmer seas worldwide, in the Atlantic and Pacific Oceans, and off the coast of Australia. It is now being farmed in the US.

Available All year round. Usually sold fresh as fillets but as cobia attract visible parasites, look carefully before buying.

Cooking Grill, poach or cube for kebabs.

Substitute Larger members of the mackerel family.

Tautog
*(alternative names black porgy,
blackfish, oyster-fish)*

Tautoga onitis

*tautogue noir, matiote (French), Austernfisch (German),
bodiao da ostra (Portuguese)*

Characteristics Plump-bodied with dark olive or brown-black skin, sometimes mottled with darker blotches, tautog is a large member of the wrasse family that can weigh up to 11kg (25lb), although 1.3kg (3lb) is average. It has a blunt nose, rubbery lips and powerful jaws for grinding its prey. The white flesh is firm, mildly flavoured and has a close, tight flake.

Habitat Living along the bottom around wrecks, piers, rocks and the mussel beds they feed on, tautog are found from Nova Scotia to South Carolina.

Available All year round, although stock levels vary and are insufficient to make tautog an important commercial fish.

Cooking Pan-fry, grill or bake and use in soups such as chowders. The skin should be removed before cooking because it has a bitter flavour.

Substitute Other species of wrasse, snapper, sea bream.

Swordfish
(alternative name broadbill)

Xiphias gladius

espadon (French), *pez espada, emperador* (Spanish), *pesce spada* (Italian),
Schwertfisch (German), *espadarte* (Portuguese)

Characteristics No one seems quite sure whether its long snout is actually used to kill other fish or just stun and confuse them but the solitary swordfish can grow to 4.5m (15ft) with the giant 'sword' adding another 1.5m (5ft). Mostly white with horizontal bands of blue or deep purple, by the time a fish is adult it has lost its teeth and scales. The pink flesh can be tinged with orange when raw but turns creamy white when cooked and dries out quickly if overdone.

Habitat Fished around the world, swordfish migrate between temperate and tropical waters and are usually caught at night when they rise to the surface to feed. Over-fishing in the late nineties led to many American chefs removing swordfish from their menus but stocks are now gradually recovering.

Available All year round. Sold in 'wheels', that display the unique whirling patterns in the flesh, these can be whole, halved or quartered. Small fish are sold cleaned and de-headed as 'logs'.

Cooking Pan-fry, grill, bake or cube for kebabs. Steaks around 2.5cm (1in) thick will have a more moist flavour than thinner ones.

Substitute Tuna, marlin.

Black oreo dory
(alternative name black dory)

Allocyttus niger

Saint-Pierre de fond de Nouvelle-Zealande (French), *omematodai* (Japanese), *deepsea dory* (New Zealand)

Characteristics Not related to the smooth oreo or John Dory. An average fish weighs around 1kg (2¼lb) and has a deep, compressed body with quite a large head and huge bug eyes. The slate-grey skin has rough scales that can't be removed and the fins are black. The off-white flesh is delicate with a mild to sweet taste; it holds together well when cooked and has a fine texture.

Habitat Native to the deep waters around New Zealand where it lives close to the seabed. A similar species is caught in South Africa.

Available New Zealand: all year round. Australia: from January to March, October to December. Small skinned fillets.

Cooking Pan-fry, grill, steam, bake and use in fish soups and stews.

Substitute John Dory.

Scabbard fish

(alternative names cutlass fish, sabre fish, silver sabre, black sabre)

Aphanopus carbo, Trichiurus lepturus

coutelas, sabre (French), *pez sable, pez cintro* (Spanish), *pesce sciabola* (Italian), *Strumpfbanfisch, Degefisch* (German), *espada branca, peixe-espada* (Portuguese), *southern frostfish* (Australia)

Characteristics There are two species of scabbard fish, silver and black, the latter being a speciality on the island of Madeira. The long, narrow body is finless and the fierce-looking mouth has sharp teeth. Most are around 90cm (3ft) long and weigh 1–2kg (2¼–4½lb). Silver scabbards have soft, delicately flavoured flesh; the black are richer and have a buttery taste.

Habitat Lives far down – as deep as 1,000m (3,000ft) – in both the cold and warm waters of the Mediterranean, Atlantic and Pacific Oceans.

Available All year round. Cutlets, steaks and fillets. Also smoked.

Cooking Bake, grill or pan-fry.

Substitute Silver scabbard: any mild-flavoured white fish. Black scabbard: mackerel.

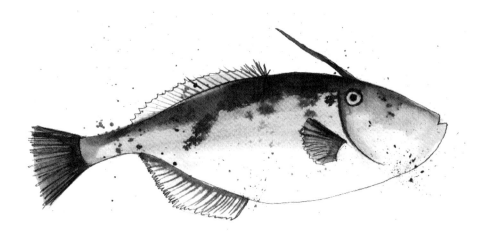

Triggerfish
(alternative name leatherjacket)

Balistes capriscus

papakol (Philippines), *usubahagi* (Japanese), *pla raet* (Thai), *barat-barat* (Malaysian),
saa maan (Hong Kong)

Characteristics Greyish brown with an oval body tapering towards the tail, the triggerfish has yellow fins and a unique single spine on its back that can be fixed in an upright position by a small 'trigger' alongside it to act as a rudimentary second backbone. Although smooth, the skin is thick and tough and usually removed before fillets of the chicken-like flesh are sold. A related species, starry triggerfish, is blue-grey to olive with numerous blue spots and three white blotches on its back.

Habitat Widely distributed across the Indian Ocean to the western Pacific through the waters of Southeast Asia, triggerfish are also found on both sides of the Atlantic and off the California coast.

Available All year round. Whole fish and fillets.

Cooking Pan-fry, grill or bake. In Malaysia the head is considered the best part to eat so the cook never removes it.

Substitute Flounder, pompano.

Garfish

(alternative names needlefish, garpike)

Belone belone

aiguile, becassine de mer, orphie (French),
agula (Spanish), *aguglia* (Italian)

Characteristics Slender and eel-like with a translucent, silver-striped body and long pointed beak, a garfish can grow to 75cm (2½ft) or more in length. Its flesh is fine-grained, soft and delicate with a mild sweet flavour and fine bones that can be eaten.

Habitat Caught around the world from the south coast of Britain, the Baltic and the eastern Atlantic to the warmer seas of Southeast Asia, southern Australia and the western Pacific.

Garfish come inshore during the summer months, living in both salt and fresh water, and inhabiting coastal waters, shallow bays and occasionally estuaries.

Available All year round but can vary according to where caught. Whole fish, chunks and skin-on fillets.

Cooking Pan-fry, grill and use in fish soups and stews.

Substitute Saury.

Flying fish

Exocoetus spp.

exocet (French), *pez volador* (Spanish), *pesce volante* (Italian),
fliegender fisch (German), *peixe-voador* (Portuguese)

Characteristics Sleek, silver-blue and looking like a giant dragonfly, the flying fish doesn't actually 'fly' but glides through the air to escape predators. Around 50 species of flying fish exist and, although larger ones are found, 30cm (12in) is an average size. The white flesh is quite compact and dry with a sweet, meaty taste once the numerous little bones have been negotiated.

Habitat Although the warm tropical and sub-tropical waters of the Atlantic, Pacific and Indian Oceans are all home to the flying fish, it is particularly associated with Barbados. It is also a staple food of the Tao people of Orchid Island near Taiwan.

Available Seasonal variations. Whole fish and fillets.

Cooking Pan-fry or steam. A local speciality in Barbados. In Japan the roe (tobiko) is used for sushi.

Substitute Another white fish such as flounder or sole fillets.

Luvar
(alternative names loo, luvaru, silver king)

Luvarus imperialis

emperador (Mexico)

Characteristics Large and solitary, the rarely seen luvar can grow to 2m (6½ft) or more and weigh 150kg (340lb). The stout, oval-shaped body is silver with salmon-pink fins, a bulging forehead and small, low-set eyes. The flesh is similar to turbot or halibut, firm and white with big succulent flakes – hence its nickname, 'the Cadillac of fish'. Its tiny, toothless mouth limits its diet to jellyfish and gelatinous plankton.

Habitat Generally lives near the surface in the tropical and sub-tropical waters of the Atlantic and Pacific Oceans and the Gulf of Mexico, although several years ago a luvar was caught in south-west England – only to be stuffed for posterity due to its rarity.

Available No regular supply. Steaks and fillets.

Cooking Pan-fry, grill, bake, steam or poach in stock or wine, using the liquid to make a sauce.

Substitute Halibut, turbot, brill.

Fugu
(alternative names blowfish, pufferfish, swellfish)

Torafugu rubripes

Characteristics There are 25 species of this fish, which has the ability to inflate into a razor-spiked ball when threatened. In Japan the rich, meaty flesh is a delicacy – despite a lethal toxin being present in the gut, liver, ovary and skin. More deadly than cyanide, the toxin has no known antidote and is unaffected by cooking. Chefs have to be highly trained to prepare it and since 1949 any restaurant selling fugu must be licensed.

Habitat Harvested mainly during the springtime spawning season and then farmed in floating cages in the Pacific. Over-fishing led to depleted stocks, resulting in restrictions, and since 2008 fish farms have been allowed to mass-produce non-toxic fugu.

Available Most expensive in winter and autmn when it is best.

Cooking Wafer thin slices of raw flesh are eaten as sashimi, followed by a main course cooked with vegetables.

Substitute None.

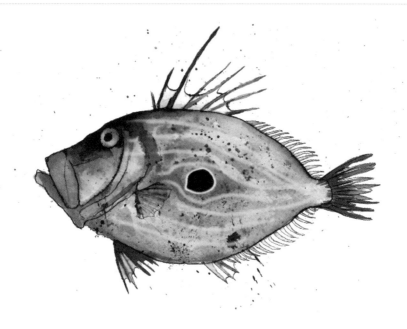

John Dory

Zeus faber

Saint Pierre (French), *pez de San Pedro* (Spanish), *pesce San Pietro* (Italian),
Petersfisch (German), *peixe-galo* (Portuguese)

Characteristics An ugly, almost prehistoric-looking fish which nevertheless has excellent flesh – firm, dense and flavoursome. The olive-yellow body – so thin it can easily hide itself from prey – has a massive head, accounting for half its weight, large retractable jaws and long spiny fins. The dark spot on its side is said to have been left there by St Peter, when the fisherman apostle caught a John Dory in the Sea of Galilee but was so filled with pity for it that he threw it back, marking its flesh with his thumbprint for eternity.

Habitat Fished from British shores to the Moroccan coast of Africa and along the Mediterranean. American dories are found in the western Atlantic but not fished commercially.

Available All year round. Whole fish and fillets – the large head reduces the edible yield to about 35 per cent.

Cooking Pan-fry, grill or steam.

Substitute Black oreo dory.

Bream

Abramis brama

breme (French), *brama* (Italian), *Bachse* (German), *brema* (Portuguese)

Characteristics Similar to sea bream but less good to eat, unless caught in clear, fresh water. Bream living in brackish water can have a muddy taste. The mild-tasting flesh is quite bony and requires strong flavours to enhance it, so serving bream plainly boiled or steamed is not recommended. Various species are found, including common, blue and white bream, all having a hump back, deep, narrow body with shiny scales, a snub nose and small mouth. An average size is around 30cm (12in).

Habitat Bream live in the lowland rivers of Europe and North America. They are also farmed.

Available Summer through to late fall for wild fish, although season depends on where caught. Farmed all year. Whole fish.

Cooking Bake, deep-fry, grill, steam, pan-fry, and serve with a sauce, or braise fish in a sauce. Difficult to fillet when very fresh.

Substitute Sea bream.

Unagi

Anguilla japonica

Characteristics Freshwater eel, known as unagi, has been a valued food since the seventeenth century in Japan, where it is looked on as a legendary source of stamina. The sweet, unctuous flesh is rich and creamy, has a pronounced fishy taste, and underlying smokiness. Traditionally eaten in Japan during the 'days of the bull', the two days after the rainy season in June, when high-energy food is needed and eel restaurants see their customer numbers soar.

Habitat Lake Hamana in Hamamatsu City is famous for being home to the finest-quality unagi and is surrounded by many small restaurants serving the local delicacy. Less highly prized eels are farmed on a large scale with more imported from China.

Available Farmed, all year round. Whole.

Cooking The most popular way to cook unagi in Japan is in the dish kabayaki, where the eel is basted with sweetened soy sauce and then grilled over charcoal, resulting in deliciously crisp skin and succulent flesh.

Substitute Other species of freshwater eel.

Whitefish

Coregonus lavaretus

coregone de lac (French), *coregono* (Spanish), *coregone dei grande laghe* (Italian), *sig* (Russian), *shiromasu* (Japanese)

Characteristics This member of the salmon family is one of the best-tasting freshwater fish. The high fat content whitefish need to survive in their icy water habitat gives the flesh a full, rich flavour and the pale orange roe is particularly prized as golden caviar. An average weight is 1–2.25kg (2¼–5lb).

Habitat Whitefish live in the cold deep-water lakes of central Europe, Scandinavia, the northern US and Canada.

Available All year round but best in winter when the flesh is firmer and plumper. Whole fish, steaks and fillets.

Cooking Bake, grill, hot-smoke, pan-fry or use in fish mousses and chowders and for fish balls. The smoked flesh is good for salads.

Substitute Salmon, sea trout.

Carp

Cyprinus carpio

carpe (French), *carpa* (Spanish, Italian, Portuguese), *Weissfische, Karpfen* (German)

Characteristics Originating from China, carp are resilient, fast-growing fish. Early merchants, many of them Jewish, brought carp back to Europe along the Silk Road so they became – and remain – a kosher favourite, notably as gefilte fish balls. Among the various species are common, mirror, grass, big-head and leather carp, all of which have tough scales, small eyes, thick lips, twin barbels on each side of the mouth and jagged spines. Common carp has a dark bronze back with gold sides and a yellow body, other species are olive green or silver-grey. The bony flesh is off-white and has a herby, almost woody flavour.

Habitat Living in temperate lakes, ponds and rivers throughout the world, any caught in stagnant waters will have a muddy taste. Farmed and pond-reared worldwide, particularly in Southeast Asia.

Available All year round. Whole fish, although fillets are sometimes available. Like bream, carp are difficult to fillet when very fresh.

Cooking Bake, steam, poach, grill, pan-fry, hot-smoke, process for fish balls or use in soup. Rinse off natural slime, and scale before cooking.

Substitute Any member of the carp family according to local availability.

Pike

Esox spp.

brochet (French), *lucio* (Spanish), *luccio* (Italian), *Hecht, Flusshecht* (German),
lucio (Portuguese), *kawakamasu* (Japanese)

Characteristics Long, slender and very savage with razor-sharp teeth and a taste for any aquatic birds or other fish brave enough to glide across its watery path. Pike flesh is firm, white, and flaky with a delicate flavour but also very bony. Weighing between 2 and 5kg (4½ and 11lb), the smaller the fish the better its flavour, as larger ones tend to be dry. When buying, look for bright silver scales, as a brownish tinge can indicate too long spent living in brackish water that will have given the flesh a muddy taste.

Habitat Pike can be found in ponds, lakes, rivers and streams from western Europe to Siberia and across the northern part of North America, where they are particularly abundant in the Great Lakes.

Available Autumn. Whole fish, steaks and fillets.

Cooking Whole fish: bake or poach. Fillets and steaks: pan-fry. Due to the many small bones, the filleted fish is often ground and made into dishes such as the French *quenelles de brochet*, which are served with crayfish-based sauce.

Substitute Trout, sea bass, grey mullet.

Catfish

Ictaluridae

wels, silure (French), *Welse, Katfisch* (German), *basa, giant Mekong catfish, pangasius* (Vietnamese), *lele* (Philippines)

Characteristics A solid, chunky, bony fish with no scales and heavy feline whiskers that poke out of its snub nose and serve as feelers in muddy water. Many species of freshwater catfish live worldwide, one of the most prolific being the American catfish, which has pink-tinged, translucent flesh that turns opaque and bright white when cooked. Others are the African catfish, boasting tough red flesh, the European Danube catfish and the giant Mekong catfish. As a general rule, the larger the fish, the coarser the flesh will be. Farmed fish are deemed to taste better than wild.

Habitat In the wild, catfish like slow-moving streams and lakes with a gravel bed but they are farmed in much of the world, including North and South America, Africa, Vietnam and Europe. The biggest recorded giant Mekong catfish, weighing 290kg (640lb), was landed by fishermen in north Thailand, the Mekong having more species of giant fish than any river on earth. King of the catfish family, however, has to be Brazil's spotted sorubim (or pintado) with its distinctive black-spotted skin and delicious bone-free flesh.

Available All year round. Fillets. The skin is tough and not eaten.

Cooking Bake, fry, and grill. The mild flesh benefits from the addition of Cajun spices or Southeast Asian seasonings.

Substitute Any members of the catfish family, salt or freshwater.

Striped bass
(alternative names greenhead, linesider, rockfish)

Morone saxatilis

bar d'Amérique (French), *lubina americana* (Spanish), *persico striata* (Italian), *Felsenbarsch* (German), *suzuki* (Japanese)

Characteristics Early settlers prized the firm, white flesh of this American species of bass for its fine flavour. The pearl in the cheek was especially well regarded for its sweetness. It has silver skin and broken black horizontal stripes running down its back and sides. Several other species of bass are found in the US.

Habitat At home in both fresh and salt water, the striped bass, like salmon, breeds in fresh. Originally fished both commercially and for sport, when stocks fell restrictions were introduced. Striped bass are now also farmed.

Available Farmed: all year round. Whole fish, fillets and steaks.

Cooking Whole fish: poach, grill or bake with a stuffing. Fillets and steaks: grill, poach, pan-fry or bake.

Substitute European sea bass.

Rainbow trout

Onorhynchus mykiss

truite (French), *truta* (Spanish, Portuguese), *trota* (Italian), *Forelle* (German)

Related species: brown, brook and golden trout. The steelhead trout is a wild, migratory species of rainbow found in the Pacific that returns to fresh water to spawn.

Characteristics One look at the sparkling silver skin, with its olive and turquoise tints and pinkish red stripe, tells you how rainbow trout got its name. Ranging in size from 225g (8oz) to 1kg (2¼lb), the flesh has a more subtle flavour than salmon. Farmed fish are fed dye to turn their flesh deep orange.

Habitat Originally found in the lakes and streams draining into the Pacific from Alaska to northern Baja Mexico and in Asia, rainbow trout are widely farmed in the US, Chile, western Europe, Argentina and Japan.

Available All year round. Whole fish and fillets.

Cooking Pan-fry, grill, bake, stuff and bake, hot-smoke or griddle.

Substitute Sea trout, salmon.

Tilapia
(alternative names St Peter's fish, sunfish)

Oreochromis spp., Tilapia spp.

tilapia du Nil (French), *tilapia del Nilo* (Spanish, Italian), *Nil-buntbarch* (German), *chikadai, terapia* (Japanese)

Characteristics Around 100 different species of tilapia exist, three of the most common being the orange, red and black, and its credentials as an eco-friendly fish are growing all the time. The lean white flesh is mild and slightly sweet, and properly farmed fish have a superior flavour to their wild cousins. Very popular in America, where most fish come from farms in Central and South America, and also in Asian cuisines.

Habitat A native of the Nile but now one of the most farmed fish in the world, a practice dating back more than 2,000 years to ancient Egypt. According to legend, it was tilapia that Jesus multiplied with the loaves to feed his followers. Hardy and adaptable, tilapia is equally at home in fresh, brackish or salt water in the wild, as it is in crowded farming aquariums.

Available All year round. Whole fish and fillets.

Cooking Pan-fry, bake or steam. The mild flesh lends itself to marinating or serving with spicy or other strongly flavoured sauces. Remove the skin because it has a bitter taste.

Substitute Flounder, sole.

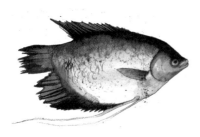

Perch

Perca spp.

perche (French), *perca* (Spanish, Portuguese), *percha, pesce persico* (Italian), *Barsch, Flussbarsch* (German)

Elephant ear fish

Osphronemus exodon

Characteristics Despite its unpromising name, elephant ear fish is renowned in Vietnam for its wonderfully sweet and succulent flesh, which is meaty, earthy and soft. A species of butterfly fish, it has a flat body, similar in shape to bass and roughly the size of a large serving platter, with a small head, big fins and silvery grey skin.

Habitat Found throughout the Mekong river delta where it is hugely popular.

Available All year round. Whole fish.

Cooking The traditional Vietnamese way is to gut and deep-fry a whole fish, then prop it up on a platter between wooden chopsticks, decorated with carved vegetables and fresh herbs. Diners use chopsticks to peel away the crisp, curling scales and reveal the flaky white flesh beneath. The flesh is then layered with local herbs such as mint, coriander and basil, and maybe noodles and cucumber, into wafer-thin rice pancakes, which are rolled up and dipped in nuoc cham fish sauce.

Substitute Bass.

Characteristics One of the best-tasting freshwater fish, perch feed on insects and fish larvae so their firm white flesh doesn't develop a muddy flavour and it also holds together well when cooked. The European perch has rough scales and is an eye-catching deep green with dark vertical bands and orange fins. Its North American cousin, the yellow perch, is smaller and lemony green with paler bands.

Habitat The European perch lives in lakes and slow-moving rivers across northern and central Europe and in Asia, and has also been introduced into Australia and New Zealand. A similar species, the Balkhash perch, is found across central Asia and China, and the yellow perch in the US and Canada.

Available All year round. Whole fish and fillets.

Cooking Grill or poach. Perch goes well with a creamy sauce such as beurre blanc.

Substitute Trout, zander.

Speckled perch
(alternative names calico bass, white perch, crappie)

Pomoxis nigromaculatus

Characteristics The state fish of Louisiana, this member of the sunfish family grows to 25–30cm (10–12in) long and commonly weighs around 900g (2lb), although fish as heavy as 1.8kg (4lb) are not unknown. Its skin is silvery olive green, mottled with darker shades, and it has a large mouth and six spines on its dorsal fin. A very good eating fish, greatly appreciated for its firm white flesh. Although known in some parts of the US as calico bass, the two are not the same: a true calico bass being a marine fish found in northeast Pacific waters.

Habitat Lives in freshwater lakes and rivers throughout the US, especially in Kansas, Ohio, Texas, the Mississippi and the bayous of Louisiana.

Available All year round. Whole fish and fillets.

Cooking Can be poached or grilled but the most popular cooking method is to deep-fry the fillets in batter.

Substitute Other species of perch, zander.

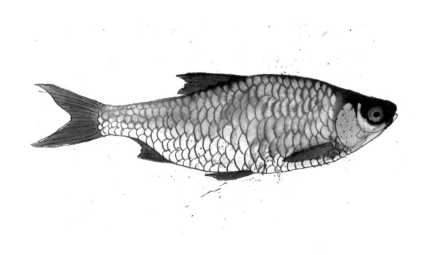

Roach

Rutilus rutilus

gardon (French), *bermejuela* (Spanish), *triotto* (Italian), *Plotze* (German), *ruivaca* (Portuguese)

Characteristics This small member of the carp family can measure as little as 5cm (2in) and rarely grows larger than 35cm (14in). It was once an important food fish in Europe, usually being preserved by drying and salting. The streamlined body has steel-blue skin with darker edged silver scales, red tinged fins and tail and a red or gold eye. The white flesh has a good flavour but is very bony.

Habitat The common roach is native to most of Europe and western Asia, where it can thrive in poor-quality shallow water, preferring weedy lakes, ponds and canals with a rocky or sandy bed. Anglers have also introduced it into Australia and Madagascar. The California roach is a different species entirely, native to western North America.

Available All year round. Whole fish.

Cooking Pan-fry. Larger fish could be grilled.

Substitute Carp.

Ishkan trout
(alternative name Sevan trout)

Salmo ischchan

Characteristics Despite its name, this unique fish from Armenia is actually a member of the salmon family. Dubbed the 'prince of fishes', reputedly because the spots on its head are said to resemble a crown, it has a silver-bronze back and spotted sides, a silver belly and small head. Its pink flesh is mild, has a delicate flavour like regular trout and is virtually boneless.

Habitat Native to Armenia's Lake Sevan, one of the largest high-altitude lakes in the world, the ishkan trout became endangered when competing species such as whitefish and Danube crayfish were introduced into the lake. It is now farmed locally and was successfully introduced into the Issyk-Kul lake in central Asia during the 1970s.

Available Farmed all year round. Whole fish.

Cooking Grill or poach. Traditional Armenian recipes include stuffing the whole fish with fruits such as prunes or apricots or oven-baking it and serving with walnut sauce.

Substitute Trout.

Arctic char
(alternative names Hudson Bay salmon, Quebec red trout, Alpine char)

Salvelinus alpinus

omble chevalier (French), *salvelino* (Spanish), *salmerino alpino* (Italian), *Saibling* (German), *eqaluc* (Greenland)

Characteristics Closely related to the salmon but smaller, this is one of the most northerly freshwater fish. Its flesh has a mild but rich flavour. Deeply embedded in the Inuit culture of Canada, where it is a staple food, in England during the 18th and 19th centuries Arctic char was considered a status symbol by the wealthy.

Habitat Fish live in both salt and fresh water, thriving in icy polar seas and returning to rivers and streams to spawn and spend the winter. Others live permanently in the landlocked lakes of Scandinavia, the Alps and the British Isles. Its extreme habitat makes commercial fishing for Arctic char difficult.

Available Farmed, year round. Wild, autumn. Whole fish and fillets.

Cooking Pan-fry, grill, bake, poach and hot- or cold-smoke. Remove the leathery skin.

Substitute Salmon, sea trout, trout.

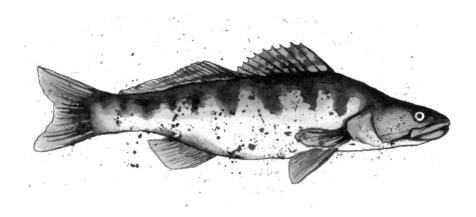

Zander
(alternative name pike-perch)

Sander lucioperca

sandre (French), *lucioperca* (Spanish, Portuguese), *sandra* (Italian), *Zander* (German)

Characteristics A member of the perch family with quite firm, meaty flesh scented with the fragrance of fresh herbs, zander challenges pike as Europe's most voracious predator. It can grow up to 90cm (3ft) long, has spiny fins, sharp teeth and two separate dorsal fins. The back is brownish green and grey, shading to white with a silvery sheen on the underside, and its mouth is large, its upper jaw extending almost to the back edge of its eye.

Habitat Zander prefer the warmer waters of Central and Eastern Europe to its icy rivers and lakes,

living in brackish water. Two close North American relatives, the brown, yellow and silver walleye and its lookalike, the sauger, are found in Canada and the US.

Available Peak season is late autumn, late winter and spring. Whole fish and fillets.

Cooking Bake, pan-fry, poach or deep-fry.

Substitute Carp.

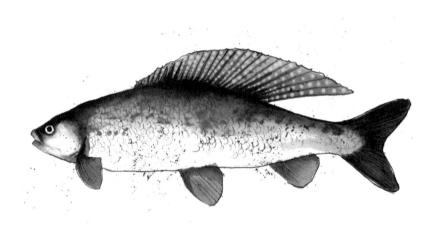

Grayling

Thymallus thymallus

Characteristics A rather bony member of the salmon family with a silver-grey back and sides that darken with age. The skin has quite large scales and shades to white on the underside. Keen noses can detect a hint of thyme scenting the firm white flesh, which is delicate and well flavoured. The grayling's most striking feature is its broad, high and colourful dorsal fin that forms a graceful cockade on its back.

Habitat Although occasionally found in lakes, grayling generally prefer the pure water of swift-running rivers with deep currents, rocks and gravel beds. Found in the UK and Scandinavia. The related *Thymallus arcticus* is a sport fish in North America.

Available From July to April. Whole fish of around 450g (1lb) and fillets.

Cooking Bake, hot-smoke or pan-fry. A traditional English country recipe suggests splashing beer over the fish, wrapping it in foil and roasting the parcel over charcoal.

Substitute Trout, salmon.

Tench
(alternative name doctor fish)

Tinca tinca
tanche (French)

Characteristics Despite its preferred muddy habitat, tench is a fine-flavoured fish and recipes making use of its gelatinous quality date back to medieval times. It has a similar body shape to carp with olive-green skin shading to gold on the belly, a square tail and small scales that are deeply embedded in the thick skin. Legend has it that any sick fish coming into contact with the tench's slimy skin would be cured, earning it the alternative name of doctor fish.

Habitat A warm-water fish that lives in brackish lakes with muddy or sandy beds and slow-moving lowland rivers throughout Europe and into western Asia.

Available All year round. Whole fish.

Cooking Grill, poach, pan-fry or bake. The 19th-century British cookery writer Mrs Beeton recommended making a fish stew of tench cut into chunks, oysters and anchovies. A French recipe poaches whole tench in Beaujolais. Rinse off slime, and scale before cooking.

Substitute Carp.

Whisker sheatfish

Micronema bleekeri

pla daeng, pla neu on (Thai)

Characteristics Very flat with no scales, this long slender fish has a humpback, small snub-nosed head, and bright silvery body that is dark along the back before shading to rainbow bands of aquamarine, lilac blue and red-gold on the belly. Feeding on shrimp roe and plankton, its flesh is rich and full flavoured and is eaten both fresh and smoked. Generally quite small, the largest recorded fish measured 60cm (2ft).

Habitat Prolific in the Mekong, Don and Chao Praya rivers of Thailand, particularly around the old city of

Ayutthaya, and in Indonesia.

Available All year round. Whole fish.

Cooking Usually deep-fried whole and served with crispy garlic and seafood sauce or curry sauce. The bones become brittle when fried and are eaten along with the rest of the fish, like potato chips.

Substitute Freshwater catfish.

Sturgeon

Acipenseridae

esturgeon (French), *esturion* (Spanish), *storeone* (Italian), *Stor, Sterlet* (German),
esturjao solho (Portuguese), *chozame* (Japanese)

Characteristics Of the 25 species of sturgeon, the most famous are those prized for their caviar – beluga, sevruga and oscietra. The European sturgeon, the North American white and green sturgeons and the small, rare, freshwater sterlet are also highly regarded. One of the oldest creatures on the planet, this long, silver grey fish with its heavy armour of bony plates rather than scales, has firm, compact flesh that is often compared to veal. Sterlet has a particularly fine flavour and a whole grilled fish was served to Presidents Putin and Bush when the latter stopped over in Moscow in 2005.

Habitat Wild European sturgeon once populated the lakes, rivers and estuaries of Russia, Siberia and the Mediterranean until the quest for caviar decimated numbers. Although some wild fish are still found in southwest France and the Black Sea, most

is now farmed. The majority of white sturgeon, North America's largest freshwater fish, found in the wide rivers of the Pacific northwest, is now also farmed.

Available Wild (in the US) summer and autumn. Farmed all year round. Small whole fish, steaks and skinless fillets

Cooking Grill, pan-fry, sear, hot-smoke or cut into wafer-thin slices and fry quickly as for veal scaloppine.

Substitute A meaty, white fish such as monkfish.

Shad

Alosa spp.

American shad: *alose savoureuse* (French), *shyado* (Japanese)

European shad: *alose vraie* (French), *sabalo commun, trisa* (Spanish), *alaccia, alosa* (Italian),

Alosa, Alse, Maifisch (German), *savel* (Portuguese)

Characteristics Similar to a chubby, greenish silver herring, the American shad has delicate, sweet flesh, its only drawback being the numerous small bones. As well as the main skeleton, shad have a second set of bones at right angles to it, making the fish difficult (and commercially expensive) to fillet, one reason why the roe is more highly rated in the US. Across the Atlantic European shad is traditionally cooked in a sorrel sauce that reputedly dissolves the tiny bones. The soft, light grey flesh has a rich, oily flavour.

Habitat American shad travel north up the Atlantic coast from Florida to Labrador in spring to spawn; on the Pacific coast they enter the Columbia river from May to July. European shad are rarely found in northern Europe, preferring the warmer waters of the Mediterranean. Other species are found around the world, many in Southeast Asian waters, including the toli, kelee, gizzard and slender shad. In Bengal shad is a particularly important food fish.

Available All year round depending on where caught. Whole fish and roe.

Cooking Pan-fry or bake, with or without a stuffing. The roe can be pan-fried in butter or olive oil.

Substitute Herring, mackerel.

Eel

....

Anguilidae spp.

anguille (French), *anguila* (Spanish), *anguilla* (Italian), *Aal, Flussaal* (German), *enguia, eiro* (Portuguese)

Varieties: European, American, short-finned (Australia/New Zealand), long-finned

Characteristics More than 20 members make up the global freshwater eel family, all being long and slender with smooth, slippery skins, minute scales and spineless fins. Their grey flesh turns off-white when cooked, and is quite firm and full-flavoured with small flakes. Tiny immature eels (elvers) are a great delicacy in Spain, where they are fried briefly in olive oil with garlic and chilli and served sizzling hot. Thinner than a pencil and transparent – their alternative name is 'glass eel' – they are eaten with a wooden fork because a metal one could spoil their mild, creamy flavour.

Habitat Both European and American eels are born in the Sargasso Sea in the Atlantic. They spend the next three years swimming back to the rivers where their parents once lived, only to return to the Sargasso to spawn once they reach maturity. Dating from prehistoric times, their migrating route is said to have followed the outer edge of the mythical city Atlantis.

Available Season depends on where caught. Farmed all year round. Whole fish, best bought live.

Cooking Braise, poach, bake or hot-smoke. Remove the skin before eating.

Substitute Any member of the eel family.

Atlantic salmon
(alternative name Baltic salmon)

Salmo salar

Pacific salmon

Oncorhynchus spp.

Characteristics There are five different species of Pacific wild salmon: chinook or Copper River king salmon is the largest and finest; coho or silver has a chubby body and deep pink flesh and is popular for cold-smoking; sockeye has deep red, lean flesh and is often tinned as 'red salmon'; chum or keta is lighter fleshed, low in fat and less highly rated; while humpback or pink is the smallest and most popular in Asia.

Habitat Wild Pacific salmon are caught from Alaska to California during a strictly controlled closed season.

Available Fishing starts in June with chinook and runs into September. Coho are also farmed in Chile, Japan and the US. Whole fish, steaks and fillets.

Cooking Poach, pan-fry, grill, hot- or cold-smoke, and use in fish mousses, pies, fishcakes and stews. The rich flesh goes well with strong Asian and Cajun flavours. Farmed salmon can be used for sushi and sashimi. The traditional accompaniment is hollandaise sauce.

Substitute Sea trout, rainbow trout, Atlantic salmon.

Characteristics Once a luxury fish available only to the wealthy. As wild salmon stocks decreased, the rise in farmed salmon has transformed it into one of the northern hemisphere's best-selling species. Large – around 15kg (34lb) when wild, 2–8kg (4½–18lb) when farmed – with silver skin dotted with black spots on the upper body and head. The plump, fatty flesh is a deep pink from the krill the fish eats and stays moist and juicy when cooked.

Habitat Wild salmon are found in limited quantities in Europe and North America, spending most of their life at sea but returning to freshwater to spawn. Overcrowded, poorly husbanded fish farms have attracted bad publicity for farmed salmon but increasingly better managed farms are producing excellent-quality fish.

Available Closed seasons for wild fish. Farmed all year round. Whole fish, steaks, and fillets.

Cooking As for Pacific salmon.

Substitute Sea trout, rainbow trout, Pacific salmon.

Smelt
(alternative names cucumber fish, candlefish)

Osmerus mordax

éperlan (French), *eperlanos* (Spanish), *eperlano* (Italian), *Stint* (German), *eperlano* (Portuguese)

Characteristics A small fish, its name is the Anglo-Saxon word for 'shiny', with tiny, soft bones. When fresh it gives off the fragrant aroma of sliced cucumber; when cooked the flesh is delicate with a fine flake. Very small fish can be eaten whole as the bones are so soft. If larger, the cooked flesh comes away easily from the bones.

Habitat In Europe smelt live in the cold northern waters around the British Isles, Normandy in France, through the Baltic to Scandinavia, and in the Bay of Biscay, migrating to lakes and rivers to spawn. The rainbow smelt and the larger, more oily Pacific or Columbia River smelt are popular in the US.

Available Winter and spring. Whole fish. Larger ones can be boned as single fillets or butterflied.

Cooking Pan-fry, deep-fry, grill, bake, barbecue or cook very small fish in the same way as whitebait.

Substitute Sprat, whitebait, sardine, herring.

Sea trout
(alternative names ocean trout, salmon trout, sewin)

Salmo trutta

truite de mer (French), *trucha marina* (Spanish), *trota di mare* (Italian), *Meerforelle, Bachorelle* (German),
truta-marisca marinha (Portuguese)

Characteristics Salmon's much sought-after smaller, wild cousin has sweet, red flesh that is midway between salmon and trout in taste and texture. Spottier and slimmer than salmon, it has a squatter tail, a body with a silvery sheen that can have a bronze hue and a long mouth that droops past its eye.

Habitat Native to the UK, sea trout are also found in Scandinavia, Iceland, the Baltic and along the European Atlantic coast as far south as Portugal. Related species are found in Chile, Argentina, Australia, New Zealand and off the eastern coast of North America. Although classified as the same species as brown trout, young sea trout (known as smolts) migrate to the sea to feed and grow before returning to fresh water to spawn, something that brown trout don't do. The spotted sea trout, *Cynoscion nebulosus*, is found along the east coast of the US and is an important sport fish in Florida.

Available The season for wild fish runs from March 1 to August 31. Sea trout are now also being farmed, which is widening their availability.

Cooking Pan-fry, grill, bake.

Substitute Rainbow trout, salmon, Arctic char.

SEAFOOD

Although, strictly speaking, fish are classified as 'seafood', when we use that term we generally mean the huge families of watery creatures made up of those with tough shells like crustaceans, molluscs and gastropods and the soft-bodied cephalopods, squid, cuttlefish and octopus. Almost prehistoric in appearance, many varieties of seafood are among the world's most prized – and most expensive – gourmet delicacies.
A grilled lobster, fresh from the sea and served with a spoonful of lemon mayonnaise is a dish fit for a king. Giant prawns sizzling on a barbecue and drizzled with lime juice will make any summer party go with a swing and moist, flaky crab cakes with a crisp crumb jacket make a memorable lunch or supper dish.

Clams

Many different types of clam are found worldwide, ranging in size from tiny to very large. Their shells, which can be either hard or thin and brittle (known as 'soft-shell clams'), consist of two, generally equal, halves joined at the base with a hinge joint. Clams can be steamed, fried, boiled, baked or eaten raw.

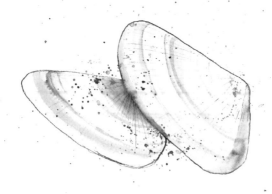

Telline de Camargue
(alternative names wedge shell, coquina clam)

Donax trunculus

telline, olive de mer (French), *coquina, tallarina* (Spanish), *tellina* (Italian), *cadelhina* (Portuguese)

A tiny, oval-shaped clam that has a shiny pale grey-beige shell and a subtle taste of the sea. Native to the Camargue region of southern France, tellines are most abundant along the coast between Montpellier and the Rhône delta south of Arles, where each morning *tellinier* fishermen gather them by using nets mounted on frames that they drag along the sandy

Mediterranean shoreline. Traditionally eaten raw, they can also be added to risottos and pasta dishes, cooked with a Provençal tomato sauce or steamed and garnished with a parsley and garlic *persillade*. A typical serving can contain up to 50 tellines.

Amande
(alternative name dog cockle)

Glycymeris glycymeris

amande de mer (French), *almendra de mar* (Spanish),
pie d'asino (Italian), *castanhola-do-mar* (Portuguese)

Dredged from the sandy seabeds of the northwest
Atlantic and the Mediterranean, amande gets its
name from the French word for 'almond', its flavour
said to resemble that of the nut. The shell is a riot of
orange, purple and white splashes and it has been
dubbed the 'poor man's oyster'. Can be eaten raw as
part of a platter of *fruits de mer*, cooked with white
wine and parsley *à la marinière*, or stuffed with
breadcrumbs, fresh herbs and garlic, and grilled.

Razor clam
(alternative name razorshell)

Ensis ensis, Ensis directus

couteau (French), *navaja, longueiron* (Spanish), *cappa lunga,*
cannolicchio (Italian), *meerscheiden, Scheiden-muschel*
(German), *longueirao, faca* (Portuguese)

Looking like something Sweeney Todd might have
wielded, this elongated clam has a fragile curved
dark green and brown shell. Found from the
Atlantic coast of Spain to Norway and in parts of the
Mediterranean, it burrows itself deep into the soft
sand exposed between low and high tide. A larger
variety – *Siliqua patula* – is also found off the Pacific
coast of the US. The muscular white meat, which
almost entirely fills the shell, is known as the 'foot'
and has a succulent sweetness that is a cross between
lobster and scallop when cooked. Razor clams can
be steamed, grilled and dressed with a herb or garlic
butter, added to chowders, pasta dishes and fritters,
but, like most shellfish, become tough and tasteless
when overcooked.

Geoduck
(alternative name king clam)

Panopea abrupta

panope (French), *Geoduck-muschel* (German),
mirugai (Japanese)

Pronounced 'gooey-duck', the name of this giant
soft-shell clam derives from a Native American word
meaning 'dig deep'. Long-lived – clocking up over
100 years – it is the largest burrowing clam and
can weigh as much as 4kg (9lb). Indigenous to the
Pacific, geoducks are harvested individually under
controlled conditions by divers who use water jets
to wash away sand and debris to reveal the clam. In
Japan, the sweet, almost crisp, neck (syphon) meat is
eaten raw in sashimi and sushi, blanched and served
with a dipping sauce, or stir-fried. In China, where it
is known as the 'elephant trunk clam', the neck meat
is dried and added to broths. In the US it is popular
in chowders and clambakes. The more tender body
meat is usually pan-fried.

Hardshell clam
(alternative names quahog,
American hardshell clam)

Mercenaria mercenaria

clam (French), *almeja, clame* (Spanish), *vongola dura,
arsella* (Italian), *Sandklaffmuschel* (German),
cadelinha (Portuguese)

This American favourite (whose alternative name is
pronounced co-hog) has a thick creamy grey shell,
can live for more than 150 years and is dredged or
racked from the sandy beds of coves and bays. Once
opened the meat must be eaten quickly to avoid any
build-up of bacteria. On the eastern seaboard of the
US, small clams called 'littlenecks', named after
Little Neck Bay on Long Island, once an important
clam centre, are usually eaten raw, while larger
'cherrystones' are stuffed and baked. They can also
be added to chowders or turned into clam juice.

Toheroa

Paphies ventricosa

Native to just a few beaches on New Zealand's North and South Islands, in particular the Muriwai and Ninety Mile beaches of north Auckland, a toheroa clam can grow up to 15cm (6in) long. It buries deep into the sand on beaches backed by dunes, where freshwater seeping from pools in the dunes supplies the plankton on which it feeds. The shell is solid, white, elongated and edged with deep electric blue. Usually chopped and added to soups or fritters, the khaki-green flesh is like a richer, creamier mussel. Now heavily protected, the smaller, more prolific tua tua (surf clam) can replace toheroa in recipes.

Surf clam

Spisula solidissima

mactre solide (French), *escupina, almeja blanca* (Spanish), *capa Americana, spisula* (Italian), *Dickschalige, Trogmuschel* (German)

Similar to hardshell clams but with a thick, triangular, yellowish white shell that is ridged with rounded edges. Surf clams live on both sides of the Atlantic, those found in the west along the New Jersey coastline being larger than ones caught in the east. Ocean dwellers, they bury themselves in coarse or fine sand. Less good than some clams to eat, they are mainly used for chowders or served deep-fried.

Giant clam

Tridacna gigas

taklobo (Philippines), *hoy mu sua* (Thai), *kimah, gebang*
(Malaysian), *wan man ho* (Hong Kong)

The largest of the bivalve molluscs, the giant clam
has a wavy-edged black and white shell and multi-
coloured yellow, white, purple and dark red flesh
that transforms it into an exotic flower when its
shell opens to feed. Tipping the scales at up to an
eye-watering 200kg (440lb) and measuring 1.2m
(4ft) across, it is native to the shallow coral reefs in
tropical seas from East Africa to Fiji. The mantle
meat bordering the shell has a good flavour and can
be steamed or curried with Thai spices. The main
part of the flesh is the most prized, being sliced,
boiled, dried and then used in soups.

Carpet shell clam

Venerupis decussata

Palourde, clovisse (Provence) (French), *almeja fina* (Spanish),
vongola verace (Italian), *Teppichmuschel* (German), *ameijoa
boa* (Portuguese)

Highly prized by French, Italian and Spanish
gourmets, this small clam with its grooved grey or
deep pink and white shell is most famous as the
essential ingredient in *spaghetti alle vongole*, the
Neapolitan pasta dish of spaghetti with steamed
clams in garlic and white wine sauce. One of the best
tasting of the smaller clams with quite meaty flesh,
its close relative, the golden carpet-shell, is even
smaller and has a vividly patterned shell of gold,
grey and white zig-zags.

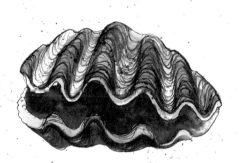

Venus clam
Venus spp.
venus (French), *almeja* (Spanish), *vongola* (Italian),
Klaffmuschel (German), *cadelinha* (Portuguese)

The Venus family of small, medium and large clams
can have round or triangular shells and range in
colour from mottled grey-white to grey and white
striped or zig-zagged in black on white, beige,
chestnut brown and dusty pink. Quite common in
Europe, they are also farmed in Mexico on the Baja
peninsula. They go well with pasta but can be quite
sandy inside so it's worth straining any sauce they
are cooked in before eating.

Praire clam
(alternative name warty Venus)
Venus verrucosa
praire (French), *verigueto* (Spanish), *tartufo di mare* (Italian),
Venusmuschel (German),
pe de burro (Portuguese)

Similar to a giant cockle with a brown-beige shell
heavily marked with concentric wart-like ridges.
Harvested from sand and gravel beds, using
sustainable methods, in the temperate waters of the
eastern Atlantic, Mediterranean and the west and
south coasts of the UK. An excellent eating clam
with a soft, silky texture and pleasantly briny flavour,
it is best served raw but can be added to risottos,
pasta dishes and paellas. The measure of how highly
Italians rate it can be seen from the translation of its
name, 'sea truffle'.

Mussels

Mussels naturally cling to rocks, piers, wooden poles and anything else they can latch onto. These days most of the best-quality mussels are rope-grown, being suspended on ropes in the water to ensure they don't touch the seabed and pick up grit and barnacles. Their blue-black shells are quite thin as they live in sheltered waters so don't need to build up a hard shell to survive in stormy seas. Rope-grown mussels are available all year round but are not at their best in summer. Cheaper, dredged mussels need to be cleaned to remove sand and grit and have less meat than rope-grown.

Before cooking, rinse mussels in plenty of fresh water and pull off any threadlike 'beard' attached to the shells. Steam them with white wine, shallots and parsley à la marinière, *in fish stock or a serving sauce, and discard any whose shells remain tightly closed as they will not be safe to eat. Larger mussels can be stuffed and grilled in the half shell or added to soups, fish pies and paellas.*

Date-mussel
(alternative names date-shell, sea date)

Lithophaga spp.

datte de mer (French), *datil de mar* (Spanish), *dattero di mare* (Italian), *Meerdattel* (German), *ishimate* (Japanese)

The rarest and most highly prized of molluscs, the date-mussel takes years to grow to its mature size of 12.5cm (5in). Long, brown-black and cylindrical, it resembles the fruit of the date palm, from which it gets its name. Native to the Mediterranean, it secretes a liquid acid that enables it to soften and then bore into the limestone rock and coral where it lives, causing considerable destruction and making it difficult to harvest without disturbing the habitats of other marine life. Highly protected, trade has shifted from western Europe, where its collection has been banned or severely curtailed, to north and east European countries. Plump and juicy, the meat is usually eaten raw. It can also be added to soups and risottos.

European mussel
(alternative name blue mussel)

Mytilus edulis

moule (French), *mejillón* (Spanish), *cozza* (Italian), *Miesmuschel* (German), *mexhilhao* (Portuguese)

Native to the Mediterranean but now farmed around the world, this small mussel has a sleek, shiny shell with plump cream and orange meat that is juicy and richly flavoured. France is famous for its blue mussels, especially those from the north Brittany coast around Mont St-Michel, where they are cooked in cider and cream, and the Ile de Ré, where they are roasted over pine needles.

New Zealand greenshell mussel
(previously called green-lipped mussel)

Perna canaliculus

moule verte (French)

This large mussel is found only in New Zealand and, although it can grow considerably bigger, commonly measures around 10cm (4in). Its vibrant dark green and gold outer shell is pearly white inside and edged with a shimmering jade band. The plump, tender flesh comes in two colours, creamy white indicating a male and apricot to orange for a female, but is equally good whatever the gender.

Oysters

Fossilised evidence points to oysters having been eaten since prehistoric times. Despite their modern image as a luxury food, for centuries they were regarded as cheap nourishment – for example, being added to a steak pie to make the meat stretch further. Their feeding habit of filtering sea water through their gills to extract plankton makes them mineral-rich. Many different species are collected in the wild or farmed.

Pacific oyster
(alternative name Japanese oyster)

Crassostrea gigas

huître crueuse (French), *ostion* (Spanish), *ostrica* (Italian), *Auster* (German), *ostra* (Portuguese)

Larger than the European native oyster and available all year round, the original home of the Pacific oyster was Asia's Pacific coast but it has since been introduced around the world into North America, Europe, Australia and New Zealand. The deeply cupped shell shades from silver-grey to gold and the oysters attach themselves to hard or rocky surfaces in shallow waters. The mild, sweet flesh is creamy white with a dark fringe and works well in cooked dishes. Steam, coat in batter and deep-fry, add to a creamy sauce, grill, bake or serve raw topped with a tangy salsa.

European native oyster

Ostrea edulis

huître plate, belon (French), *ostra plana* (Spanish), *ostrica* (Italian), *Auster* (German), *ostra* (Portuguese)

Considered by connoisseurs to be the finest oyster there is, the European native oyster is in season in the UK from September to April. Found around the British Isles, with the main stocks in the west of Scotland and the southeast of England, it lives in shallow coastal waters on a rocky or firm muddy bed. The off-white, yellowish green shell is banded with blue and brown and is pearly white or bluish grey inside. Oval or pear-shaped, the shell has a rough scaly surface, one half of it being cup-shaped, the other flat. Native oysters have a fresh, strong briny flavour with a nutty aftertaste and are best eaten raw with just a squeeze of fresh lemon juice. Various species of native American or Eastern oysters are found from New Brunswick to the Gulf of Mexico, and European native oysters are now being farmed in Maine.

Hooded oyster

Saccostrea cucullata

talaba (Philippines), *hoy nangrom pak jaeb* (Thai),
tiram batu (Malaysian), *mau lai* (Hong Kong)

Growing up to 10cm (4in) long, this oyster, with pink
or purple circles around the edge of its black shell,
is popular in Thailand, Malaysia and Indonesia. Its
delicate sweet-salty flavour means it can be eaten
raw with a squeeze of lemon or lime juice or used in
cooked dishes.

Sydney rock oyster

Saccostrea glomerata

Native to Australia but related to the hooded oyster,
the Sydney rock oyster has been commercially
cultivated since the 1870s. Beds are found along the
coasts of Victoria, New South Wales, Queensland and
at Albany in Western Australia. Medium-sized, the
Sydney rock oyster is plump, creamy and sweet with
a salty aftertaste. Mostly eaten raw, it can also be
added to cooked dishes such as gratins or soups.

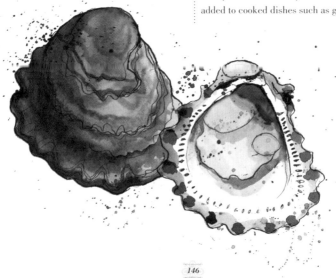

Scallops

Scallops are recognisable by their large oval white shells that have deep ribs radiating from the base with bands of orange and brown. The shell is the symbol of pilgrims who follow the route of St James to his tomb in Santiago de Compostela in Galicia and it was immortalised by Botticelli in his painting **The Birth of Venus.** *To prepare scallops, simply pull off the thin rubbery band and grey vein that is wrapped around the white nut of flesh.*

Queen scallop
(alternative name queenie)

Aequipecten opercularis
petoncle, vanneau (French), *volandeira* (Spanish), *canastrello liscio* (Italian),
Kamm-muschel (German), *vieira* (Portuguese)

Small and deliciously sweet, these baby scallops have colourful shells that shade from light pink to reddish brown. They live around the British and Irish coasts and are also farmed in Scotland. They are particularly associated with the Isle of Man, off the northwest coast of the UK, where in August 2008 the first annual Queenie Festival was held, and where they are now dredged under controlled conditions to preserve stocks. Queen scallops can be added to chowders, fish pies and salads or wrapped in bacon and griddled.

Bay scallop

Argopecten irradians

peine baie de l'Atlantique, pecten (French), *peine caletero* (Spanish), *canestrello Americano, ventaglio* (Italian), *Karibik-pilgermuschel* (German), *vieira de baia* (Portuguese)

Native to the Atlantic coast of the US, the bay scallop is the state shell of New York State. Although its wild habitat stretches from the shallow coastal waters of New England to the Gulf of Mexico, farming is on the increase, with a large proportion of those sold in the US now coming from Chinese fish farms. Small, tender and delicately sweet, bay scallops can be eaten raw, seared briefly in a hot pan, threaded onto kebabs and grilled, or added to soups and other cooked dishes. In the US the orange coral is not usually eaten.

European sea scallop

Pecten maximus

coquille St-Jacques (French), *viera* (Spanish), *ventaglio-pettine maggiore* (Italian),
Kamm-muschel, Pilger-muschel (German), *viera* (Portuguese)

Hand-harvested by divers in the waters of the eastern Atlantic from Norway to southern Spain and around the Azores. Divers pick the biggest scallops, which command a higher price than those caught by dredging, which vary in size and can be full of sand and grit from the dredging process. They are also used for the classic French dish *coquilles St Jacques à la Parisienne*. Both the white muscle meat and the orange roe can be eaten.

Cockle

Cerastoderma edule

coque (French), *berberecho* (Spanish), *cuore edule* (Italian), *Herzmuschel* (German),
berbigao (Portuguese)

The common cockle cooked and seasoned with malt vinegar and white pepper is a popular seaside snack in the UK, and when fried with bacon and laver bread makes a traditional Welsh breakfast. The rounded, heart-shaped shell shades from off-white to grey and is marked with deep ribs. The plump flesh is salty and succulent and can replace clams in any recipe. Cockles are collected by being raked from the sands at low tide, one of the main centres in the UK being Morecambe Bay in Lancashire. The north Norfolk village of Stiffkey (pronounced Stewkey) is home to a highly regarded cockle with a distinctive bright blue shell. Other species live around the world, including China's blood clam, so called because it exudes a dark red, blood-like juice.

Turu

Teredo spp.

A delicacy found only in the Amazonian rainforest, although similar species live in mangrove swamps elsewhere, the taste of this freshwater mollusc is somewhere between a sea urchin and an oyster. Long and milky grey with sharp teeth on its shell, it can grow up to 40cm (16in) in length and great skill is needed to extract it from the water. The thick flesh can be seasoned with lime, salt and chilli and served as ceviche or made into a broth.

Abalone
(alternative name sea-ear)

Haliotis spp.

ormeau (French), *oreja de mar* (Spanish), *orechia marina*
(Italian), *Seeohr* (German), *orelha* (Portuguese), *awaby,*
tokobushi (Japanese), *muttonfish, muttonshell* (Australia),
paua (New Zealand)

The abalone clings firmly to rocks with its broad
muscular foot, its domed, ear-shaped outer shell
edged with a semi-circle of fine holes. Hidden inside
the shell is an iridescent mother-of-pearl lining
that can be silvery white, pinky mauve or deep red,
depending on the species. Around 100 types of wild
abalone are found worldwide, with about 15 being
farmed. Like octopus, the flesh of a large abalone can
be tough unless given a good bashing to tenderise it.
It has a moist, delicate flavour and texture suitable
for stir-frying, adding to fish stews or eating raw
as sashimi.

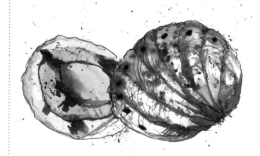

Whelk
(alternative name dog whelk)

Buccinum undatum

bulot, buccin, escargot de mer (French), *bocina,*
caracola (Spanish), *buccina* (Italian), *buzio* (Portuguese),
bai (Japanese)

Looking like a big garden snail with a grubby, off-
white shell and two 'horns', a whelk glides over the
seabed using its wide, flat, black-speckled foot to
propel it along. Whelk shells are in great demand
as a refuge for hermit crabs, the whelk and the
newcomer happily cohabiting side by side in the
same shell. The European common whelk is found
all around the British Isles. In the US, the larger,
longer, channelled and knobbed whelks are more
popular. The flesh has a pronounced briny flavour
similar to clams.

Winkle
(alternative name periwinkle)

Littorina littorea

bigorneau, lottorine, vignot (French), *bigaro* (Spanish),
chiocciola di mare (Italian), *Strandschnecke* (German),
borrelho (Portuguese)

Once beloved by London cockneys, whose treat for
Saturday night tea was a pint of winkles extracted
with a pin and sprinkled with malt vinegar. Since
then, like many cockneys, winkles have moved up
in the world and can now be found as pre-dinner
nibbles in smart establishments. Living on rocky
shores where there are plenty of algae, on both sides
of the Atlantic, the round, spiral-shaped shell can
vary from blue-black through shades of red-brown
to olive green. Boil winkles in heavily salted water
for 5 minutes, rinse under cold water to stop them
becoming tough, and remove from their shells with
a toothpick. Serve as a snack dressed with a wine
vinegar or lemon juice vinaigrette.

Murex
(alternative name rock snail)

Murex spp.

rocher épineux (French), *canadilla* (Spanish), *murice
commune* (Italian), *Herkuleskeule* (German),
buzio (Portuguese)

Hundreds of different species of this whelk-like sea
snail are found in North America, the Mediterranean
and the tropical waters of the Indo-Pacific. Their
pointed, rounded shells vary in size from 2.5–25cm
(1–10in); they have brightly coloured insides and
many are adorned with an elaborate array of spines.
The plump, sweet flesh can be made into fritters
or eaten raw as part of a platter of *fruits de mer*. An
intense purple mucus collected from a vein in the
Mediterranean murex was once used in Jerusalem's
ancient temple to dye the robes of the high priest.

Limpet

Patellogastropodae

bernique, chapeau chinois, patelle (French), *lampa*
(Spanish), *patella* (Italian), *Schusselmuschel* (German), *lapa*
(Portuguese), *opihi* (Hawaii)

Small, with a broad conical shell, limpets can be
found clamped to algae-covered rocks the world over.
Considered a great delicacy in Hawaii and Portugal,
a strong penknife is the only way to prise a limpet
from its rock. The flesh is well flavoured but quite
chewy. Boil limpets for just a couple of minutes
until they slip from their shells. Once cooked, dress
with garlic butter, vinegar, salt and pepper, or add
to a fish stew.

Conch

Strombus gigas

lambi, strombe rose (French), *cobo rosado* (Spanish),
Schneckenmuschel (German), *sazae* (Japanese)

Pronounced 'konk', this large salt-water gastropod
drags itself along the seabed with the help of its big,
edible muscular foot. Over 70 species are found in
the Indian and Pacific Oceans and the warm waters
surrounding the Caribbean islands. The most famous
– and most beautiful – queen conch, with its pointed
golden brown shell lined with deep pink pearl, is
now an endangered species and is mostly farmed.
Wild conch meat can be tough but farmed is more
tender, although less full-flavoured. Use the chopped
flesh in fritters, chowders, gumbos or salads, or cut
into strips and stir-fry or steam.

Top-shell

Trochus spp.

bigorneau (French), *caracol gris* (Spanish), *chiocciola marina* (Italian),
hoy ud (camel) (Thai), *sek tao law* (Hong Kong)

Named for its resemblance to a child's spinning top, many species are distributed throughout Europe, the tropical waters of the west Pacific, around Australia, and through Southeast Asia. Some can measure up to 15cm (6in), although the majority are much smaller, the most striking being the black and white banded zebra top-shell. The meat is chewy and has a similar flavour to abalone. Boil top-shells before extracting their flesh and use it in salads, soups and stir-fries, or serve with a sauce.

Crustaceans

A crustacean's tough outer shell has one drawback in that it doesn't grow bigger along with the creature inside. Several times during its life the crustacean is therefore forced to shed its outgrown shell and spend a short time in a vulnerable soft-shell state, floating near the surface of the water until a replacement hard shell can grow to protect it.

Live crustaceans are varying shades of dark green, blue and brown but these colours break down during the cooking process and only a carotenoid pigment in their shells remains stable, turning the cooked carapace pink or orange-red.

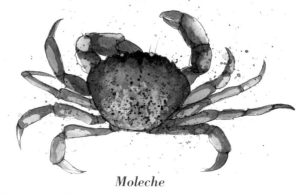

Moleche

Carcinus aestuarii

Take a trip to Venice's Rialto fish market in spring or fall and little moleche crabs will be a common sight, as will crisp *moleche frite* on local restaurant menus. These soft-shell or 'green' crabs are caught in nets along the channels of the Venetian lagoon from February to late April or early May and again in October and November. First soaked in beaten egg, they are then dusted with flour and deep-fried until crunchy on the outside and soft inside. Eaten whole in Venice, on the island of Murano the legs are usually removed and just the body eaten.

Blue crab

Callinectes sapidus

crabe bleu (French), *cangrejo azul* (Spanish), *granchio nuotore*
(Italian), *Blaukrabbe* (German),
nalvalheira azul (Portuguese)

Chesapeake Bay in the US has long been famous for
its blue crab fishery. Having an olive-green top shell
with white underneath, most crabs are caught as
hard-shells but during its two- to three-year lifespan,
the crab sheds its shell around 20 times when it can
be eaten as soft-shell.

Jonah crab
(alternative name Atlantic Dungeness)

Cancer borealis

tourteau-jona (French), *cangrejo* (Spanish), *granciporro*
atlantico rosso (Italian), *Jonahkrabbe* (German), *sapateira*
boreal (Portuguese), *kani* (Japanese)

Closely related to both peekytoe and Dungeness
crabs, the Jonah crab has an oval, orange-red top
shell with white underneath. The meat from its large
strong claws is highly regarded, with more and more
top US chefs featuring it on their menus.

Peekytoe crab
(alternative names bay crab, rock crab)

Cancer irroratus

tourteau poinclos (French), *jaiba de roca amarilla* (Spanish),
granciporro atlantico giallo (Italian), *Felsenkrabbe* (German),
sapateira de rocha (Portuguese)

Peekytoe, or 'picked toe', is the Maine slang for
'pointed' and refers to the sharp points on the crab's
legs that turn inwards. The peekytoe's delicate, sweet
pink flesh is perfect for salads and seafood cocktails.

Dungeness crab
(alternative name San Francisco crab)

Cancer magister

dormeur du Pacifique (French), *cangrejo Dungeness*
(Spanish), *granchio* (Italian), *Pazifischer*
Taschenkrebs (German)

A plump, heavy crab with beautifully sweet flesh,
sustainably fished from California to Alaska. A
typical crab weighs 900g (2lb) and the shell is
packed with meat.

Brown European crab
(alternative name common crab)
Cancer pagurus
tourteau, crabe dormeur (French), cambero masero, buey
(Spanish), granciporro, favollo (Italian), Taschenkrebs
(German), caranguejo moure (Portuguese)

Mainly caught in baited pots, brown crabs are found
all over the eastern Atlantic, the North Sea and the
Mediterranean but the best are those from the south
coast of England and around the Channel Islands.

Snow crab
(alternative name tanner crab)
Chionoecetes opilio
Eismerkrabbe (German), zuwaigani (Japanese),
queen crab (Canada)

Three varieties of this member of the spider crab
family are caught in the cold waters of the north
Atlantic and Pacific Oceans from Newfoundland
to Greenland to the Arctic tip of Norway, and from
Alaska across the Pacific to the Sea of Japan. The
snow crab has long spindly legs and a round body
that comes to a broad point at the head. The delicate,
quite firm meat has a chewy texture and ranges from
snow white to orange-brown.

Yellow oil crab
Eriocheir sinensis

Rich and buttery flavoured, yellow oil crab is in
season for a short time each summer. When fat
and ready to mate, the female mud crab lies in the
sun on the beaches at the mouth of the Pearl River
near Hong Kong and literally gets scorched. The
blazing sun melts the fat in her roe to yellow oil
that permeates and flavours her whole body. Careful
cooking is necessary to prevent the roe spilling out of
the body, so crabs are usually steamed or simmered.
Farming, which involves baking the crabs under hot
lamps, has extended the yellow oil crab season but at
the cost of quality, connoisseurs complain.

Sawagani

Geothelphusa dehaani

Fast food Japanese-style, bags of these tiny river crabs, fried whole, are sold on street stalls across Japan. Also eaten with sushi, they measure just 2cm (¾in) across, weigh a feather-light 28–42g (1–1½oz) and are found in streams throughout the country. In season during summer and autumn, they are available frozen all year and are occasionally found in Japanese restaurants worldwide.

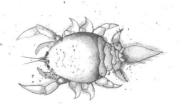

Sea cicada

Ibacus peroni

undur-undur (India), *chat chan thaley* (Thai)

This tiny crab, 3–6.5cm (1½–2½in) in length, is found in Southeast Asia, where high tides sweep them up onto beaches. The trick is to catch them as soon as they land, before they can hide in the sand. They have whitish yellow bodies with two antennae and five pairs of legs, only two of which protrude from the shell. The most popular way to cook them is to cut off the head, remove the shell and deep-fry tempura-style.

Beetle crab

(*alternative name horseshoe crab*)

Limulus polyphemus

mimi, ikan mimi (India), *maeng da* (Thai), *keroncho, belangkas* (Malaysian)

Caught in special bamboo nets in shallow water near the beach, the beetle crab has a large rounded outer shell and small black eyes. Popular in Thailand, where they are cooked with sugar and coconut or made into a soup with pineapple, the eggs are also considered a delicacy,

Spider crab

Maia squinado

araignée de mer (French), *centolla* (Spanish), *maia, granseola* (Italian), *Troldkrabbe* (German), *santola* (Portuguese)

Various species of this crab live on seabeds around the world. The thin legs and compact, relatively small body make spider crabs fiddly and time-consuming to prepare but its sweet, melt-in-the-mouth flesh makes the effort worthwhile.

Stone crab

Menippe mercenaria

Its large, meaty claws are the Florida stone crab's
main attraction. During the open season of mid
October to mid May, fishermen harvesting stone
crabs break off one claw and put the rest of the crab
back in the water – the claw will regrow and must
measure 7cm (2¾in) before it can be taken. The crab
is found in the western Atlantic from North Carolina
to Belize, in oyster beds, reefs and rocky areas.

King crab

Paralithodes camtschatica

crabe royal (French), *Kurzschwanz-krebs* (German),
tarabagani (Japanese)

Introduced into the Barents Sea during the 1960s
from Russia's Kamchatka Peninsula and Alaska, the
king crab is popular in North America and is starting
to appear in European restaurants. Unlike most crabs
that have 10 legs, this giant, which can weigh 5kg
(11lb) or more, has six long, gangly walking legs.

Hairy crab
*(alternative names Chinese mitten crab, big
binding crab)*

Pilumnus hirtellus

da zha xie, Shanghai mao xie (China)

Native to East Asia, the Shanghai hairy crab gets its
name from the long, fine hairs covering its claws. It
has little meat and is mainly eaten for its roe, which
is soft and creamy (the male 'roe' is actually its
genitals). The best hairy crabs are said to come from
Yang Cheng Lake in Jiangsu province.

Blue swimmer/swimming crab
(alternative name flower crab)

Portunus pelagicus

alimasag (Philippines), *pu ma* (Thai),
ketam renjong (Malaysian), *far haai* (Hong Kong), *yuan hai
suo zi xie* (China)

Caught around the Pacific Rim, the blue swimmer's
succulent meat is pasteurised, chilled, exported
around the world and turned into excellent crab
cakes, chowders, salads and risottos. The male crab
is light blue, the female brown, both with white spots.
In its soft state after moulting, it can also be eaten
whole. In Thailand the meat is fried, cooked with rice
to make a soup or candied and eaten as a snack.

Spanner crab
(alternative names frog crab, red frog crab)

Ranina ranina

Vivid orange or deep red in colour, the front legs
are spanner-shaped while the rest are flattened and
covered in short, spiky bristles. The spanner is noted
for its unusual forwards and backwards gait. Living
off the east and west coasts of Australia, it spends
most of the day buried in the soft, inter-tidal sand of
sheltered bays and beaches, emerging at speed when
a potential meal of small crustaceans appears. Used
in soups, salads and for making croquettes.

Mud crab
(alternative names mangrove, muddy, or black crab)

Scylla serrata

kepiting (India), *alimangong palaisdaan* (Philippines),
chang haai (Hong Kong), *xun, qing xie* (China)

A large, smooth-shelled crab found in the estuaries
and mangrove forests of Africa, Asia and Australia
that has delicate, moist flesh and is eaten both as
a hard-shell crab and, during its moulting season,
as 'soft shell'. Particularly popular in Queensland,
where it is widely farmed.

Squat lobster

Galathea squamifera

Not a true lobster at all, as the 'squat' is more closely related to crabs. Around 70 species are found worldwide, often sitting on the tops of coral reefs waiting for prey to swim past. One species thrives off the northwest coast of Scotland and around the Orkney Islands but was overlooked for years in favour of the langoustine, with which the squat lobster is often confused. Scottish squat lobsters are only 4cm (1½in) long but larger species reach 10–15cm (4–6in) and all have very long front claws. The tail contains little meat, but what there is is very sweet, juicy and pleasingly chewy. Dark brown or red and blue when live, the shell turns reddish brown when cooked. A species caught off the coasts of Chile and popular in the US is known as langostino.

American or Canadian lobster

Homarus americanus

homard Américain (French), *iseebi* (Japanese)

One of the few foods sold live in US markets, American lobsters live in shallow rocky waters from Labrador to North Carolina but the most famous and highly regarded come from Maine, where the first recorded catch dates back to 1605. Once so abundant that lobsters were regarded as poor man's food, their steady march up the culinary pecking order has forced authorities to introduce conservation methods, including minimum size limits. Sold mostly hard-shell, soft-shell lobsters can be found and are said to have sweeter meat. Harvested from July to October, most have dark brown shells when alive but rare blue and yellow lobsters are not unknown.

European lobster

Homarus gammarus

homard Européen (French), *bogavante* (Spanish), *astice* (Italian), *Hummer* (German), *lavagante* (Portuguese)

The European lobster lives mainly off the coasts of
Scotland, Ireland and western France but can also
be found as far south as the Mediterranean. Smaller
than its American counterpart, the European lobster
has a brightly speckled blue-black body and is most
abundant during the summer months. In the winter
the cold makes the lobster's metabolism slow down
so much it grows too sluggish to be tempted into a
pot. The Chinese call the European lobster by the
delightfully descriptive name 'dragon prawn'.

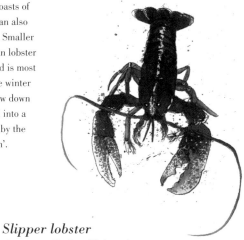

Slipper lobster
(alternative name flathead lobster)

Scyllarides latus

cigale, petite cigale (French), *cigarra de mar, santiaguino* (Spanish), *cicala di mare, magnosella* (Italian),
Barenkrebs (German), *cigarra do mar, lagosta da pedra* (Portuguese)

Another lobster family imposter, the slipper is more
closely related to the seawater crayfish or spiny
rock lobster. Its flattened body and large, plate-like
antennae give it a prehistoric appearance, but its
sweet, almost spicy tail meat more than compensates
for any deficiencies it might have in the looks
department. Found in warm waters around the world,
where it often clings to the roofs of shallow caves or
the underside of plate coral. Although very similar to
Australia's Moreton Bay and Balmain bugs, slipper
lobsters can be distinguished by their more robust
front legs.

Brown prawn
(alternative names common prawn, Morecambe Bay prawn)

Crangon crangon

crevette grise (French), *quisquilla* (Spanish), *gamberetto grigio* (Italian), *Garnele, Granat,*
Speisekrabbe (German), *camarao negro* (Portuguese)

A small brown prawn that is found on intertidal sand and mud flats around the British Isles and along the coastline of northwest mainland Europe. Cooked brown prawn can be eaten whole, shell included, but they are particularly associated with Morecambe Bay off the Lancashire coast of England, where 'potted prawns' (boiled prawn, peeled and packed in small pots with butter, pepper and nutmeg) are a local delicacy. Long and thin with a mottled brown carapace and fanned tail, the brown prawn has a sweet–salty flavour and unique chewy texture.

Banana prawn
(alternative name cat prawn)

Fenneropenaeus merguiensis

udang putih (India), *hipon buti* (Philippines), *tenjika kuruma ebi* (Japanese), *kung chabauy* (Thai)

A warm-water prawn that can reach 24cm (9½in) in length and has a creamy yellow body dotted with tiny red spots. Its legs and tail fan are also red and its flesh has an excellent flavour and firm texture. The main species of prawn farmed in Thailand, it is also an important commercial prawn in Queensland Australia. Closely related to the white prawn, which has an off-white body with blue or brown markings and reddish blue tail fan and legs. The latter is fished in many countries from Bangladesh to the Philippines, both offshore and in pond culture.

Pitu
(alternative names camarao, poti, canela, camarao verdadeiro)

Macrobrachium carcinus

This king of freshwater prawns, with its formidable claws and meaty body, lives in Latin America's estuaries and rivers, most frequently in Brazil where its image graces the bottles of one of the country's leading brands of the local sugar cane spirit, *cachaça*. A pitu's colour varies according to where it lives; at times it can be almost translucent, at others it can range from terracotta to spice brown. Less briny and more delicately flavoured than saltwater prawns, pitu grow to 27cm (10½in) long and can weigh a staggering 400g (14oz). Grill, barbecue or chop the meat and add it to traditional Brazilian stews such as *escaldados* or *moquecas*.

Hawaiian blue prawn
(alternative names giant freshwater prawn, giant river prawn, Malaysian prawn)

Macrobrachium rosenbergii

bouquet, chevrette géante (French), *langostino de rio* (Spanish), *Rosenberg-garnele* (German), *camarao gigane do rio* (Portuguese), *onitenagaebi* (Japanese)

One of over 200 species of freshwater prawn, the Hawaiian blue can weigh 100g (4oz) or more, has long legs and antennae and a bright blue tail. Fished wild throughout the Indian and Pacific Oceans, it is most abundant in summer. It is also farmed in California, the West Indies, Southeast Asia and Hawaii. Its firm flesh has a satisfyingly sweet flavour.

Black tiger prawn
(alternative name giant tiger prawn)

Penaeus monodon

udang windu (India), *ushi ebi* (Japanese),
kung kula-dum (Thai)

The largest warm-water marine prawn, the giant
black tiger can grow to an astonishing 32.5cm (13in),
although most members of the tiger prawn family are
smaller. Light brown to grey-blue and banded with
purple, black or grey, it ranges from the Red Sea
and East Africa through Southeast Asia to Australia
and is widely farmed throughout Asia. Other species
of tiger prawn include green, white and common,
and also the king prawn, which is known as the
blue-legged king prawn in Australia because its
legs and tail fan tip are mostly blue. Freshly caught
and cooked wild tiger prawns have a vastly superior
flavour to most of the farmed, particularly those that
have been frozen, which can be soft and bland.

European common prawn

Palaemon serratus

crevette rose, bouquet (French), *camaron, quisquilla*
(Spanish), *gambero* (Italian), *Krabbe, Garnele* (German),
camarao (Portuguese)

An inshore dweller, the common prawn can be found
walking towards the beach in search of food from
Norway and the north Atlantic to southern Europe.
Pale and translucent when raw, it turns a vivid
salmon red when cooked. Larger species of common
prawn also occur through the warmer waters of the
Mediterranean, including the *carabinero*, which is
one of the tastiest and is known in Cadiz as 'chorizo'
after the red juices that run out of it.

Arctic prawn
(alternative names northern prawn, pink
prawn, deep-water prawn)

Pandalus borealis

Smaller, sweeter and meatier than many of its
cousins, the pink prawn inhabits clean, icy,
unpolluted northern waters. Harvested mainly
around Canada and Greenland, it is also found in
the north Atlantic and north Pacific Oceans. A cold
environment means it matures more slowly than
warm-water prawns, which improves the flavour and
texture of its flesh. Fears of over-fishing have led to
controls being put in place. Pink prawn are popular
in Scandinavia, where they are traditionally eaten
at midsummer with a shot of aquavit. Best cooked
simply or added to a shellfish cocktail or salad.

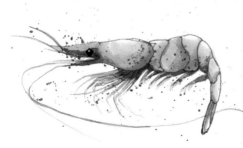

Rock prawn
(alternative name brown rock prawn)

Sicyonia brevirostris

boucot ovetgernade (French), *camaron de piedra* (Spanish), *Furchen-geisselgarnele* (German)

A native of north and central America, the rock prawn is trawled from Virginia in the southern US to Mexico's Yucatan peninsula. Named for its extremely hard pink-beige shell, the rock prawn is most abundant during late summer and fall. Despite it being dismissed as 'popcorn' prawn and a chain restaurant speciality, it has fairly firm, almost lobster-like, sweet flesh. Its hard carapace makes it so difficult to peel it was only after a special gadget was invented to split the flesh and devein the prawn that it became a commercial success. Most rock prawn is sold ready-peeled.

Mantis prawn
(alternative names sea scorpion, sea locust)

Squilla mantis

mante, squille (French), *galera* (Spanish), *cannochia, pannocchia* (Italian), *Heuschreckenkrebs* (German),
zagaia-castanheta (Portuguese), *shako* (Japanese)

Neither a praying mantis nor a prawn, this creature gets its name for looking like a combination of the two. Around 400 species exist worldwide and some can grow as large as 30cm (12in). Difficult to catch as it moves so fast, the mantis prawn leads a solitary existence buried in sand or tucked into the crevices of reefs and rocks. Its translucent shell can vary from dull brown or grey to fluorescent shades of green, mauve or pink. Dubbed 'thumb splitters' by divers for their viciously strong claws that can smash prey and even crack aquarium glass, their firm flesh tastes closer to lobster than prawn. Popular in Mediterranean countries, particularly northern Italy, they can be fried, stewed, used in fish soups or grilled. In Japan they are eaten as sashimi.

Yabby

Cherax destructor

'Yabbying' is a popular pastime for children in Australia, where they tie a lump of meat to a length of string, dangle it in the water and wait for a yabby to bite. Various species are found in swamps, rivers and farm dams, most prolifically in Victoria, New South Wales and south Queensland. A common size is 10–20cm (4–8in), although yabbies can grow as large as 30cm (12in) and can survive long periods of drought by burrowing into muddy, swampy beds.

Marron

Cherax tenuimanus

Rated by many as the best eating crayfish there is, marron is native to Western Australia's Margaret River. Both smooth and hairy species are found in the wild but only in a very small area, so fishing is tightly regulated. Farming has increased the supply, particularly around Kangaroo Island off the coast of South Australia, some of the best being exported live, as freezing is not recommended. The name comes from the Aboriginal word 'nyungar', meaning bread or food. Marron is the world's third largest crayfish and can weigh up to 2kg (4lb). Dark brown when alive, it turns vermilion when cooked. The body and claws have plenty of white, red-tinged, sweetly scented meat that has a nutty flavour, the claw meat being particularly good.

European crayfish
(alternative names signal crayfish, redclaw)

Astacus astacus

Hailing from the western US, a European crayfish can grow to about 15cm (6in) in length and survive for long periods out of water, allowing it to travel across land between watery habitats. A solitary creature that will eat anything from vegetation to smaller crayfish, it has a greenish brown hard carapace when alive, large claws and a deep orange undershell, and turns deep scarlet when cooked. The claws have little meat but can be used to make full-flavoured stock. The tail meat is juicy and succulent.

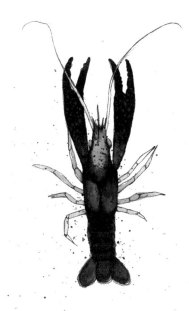

Crayfish
(alternative names crawfish, crawdad)

Procambarus clarkii

The red- and white-river crayfish from northern Louisiana are the most important farmed species in the US, the state being home to 90 per cent of America's freshwater crayfish. Popular in Creole and Cajun cuisines, the traditional way to eat these swamp dwellers is as 'crawfish boil', where they are cooked in a large pot with spices and eaten with the hands at long tables covered with newspaper. Reddish black when alive but turning deep lobster red when cooked, their white meat is covered with a brownish red membrane and is similar in flavour to lobster, but less dense.

Spiny lobster
(alternative names crawfish, rock lobster)

Palinuridae

langouste (French), *langosta* (Spanish), *aragosta* (Italian),
Languste (German), *lagosta* (Portuguese)

Missing the large claws of a true lobster, the spiny lobster is nevertheless prized for its firm, rich, red-tinged tail meat, which makes up a third of its body weight. Around 30 species are found worldwide, the most significant being the European, which is caught off the rocky coasts of Ireland, southwest England, Brittany in France and Galicia in Spain; the Baja blue from the Mexican Pacific coast; and those from the Caribbean, California, Australia, Brazil, New Zealand and South Africa. Tails from spiny lobsters caught in cold waters tend to have a better flavour than those from warmer waters.

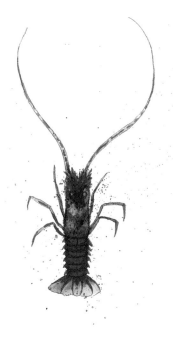

Langoustine
(alternative names Dublin Bay prawn, scampi, Norway lobster, lobsterette)

Nephrops norvegicus

langoustine (French), *cigala, langostina* (Spanish), *scampi* (Italian), *Kaisergranat,*

Norwegischer Schlankhummer (German), *lagostim* (Portuguese)

The turbulent cold seas of the Corryvreckan 'whirlpool' between Scotland's west coast and the Inner Hebrides, is home to what many consider to be the finest crustaceans in the world. Here the native langoustines are trapped like lobsters in pots and can reach up to a mighty 450g (1lb) in weight. Smaller, less highly prized langoustines are caught off the coasts of Europe in nets and weigh only about 28–42g (1–1½oz). Slim and orange-pink with two long pointed claws, only the tail meat, which has a unique sweet flavour, is eaten.

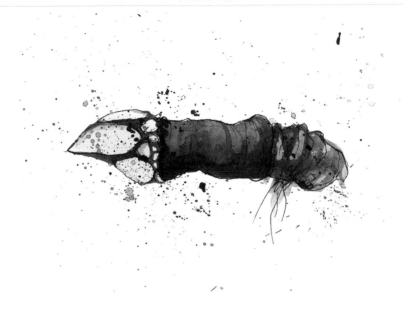

Goose-necked barnacle

Pollicipes polymerus

pouce-pied (French), *percebe* (Spanish), *balano, lepade cornucopia* (Italian),
Felsen-entenmuschle (German), *perceve* (Portuguese)

A crustacean that looks and lives like a mollusc, the goose-necked barnacle is particularly prized in Spain, where in Galicia a festival is held each year in its honour. Not to everyone's taste, critics have likened the slippery, chewy flesh to tripe, despite its lobster-like flavour. Found in colonies that cling to rocks along the ocean's foamy edge, the barnacle has a fan-like, feathery foot, a long soft body said to resemble the neck of a goose and a pair of bony white plates on top. To feed, it needs rolling surf to deliver its diet of plankton. Often served in clusters, the barnacles can be eaten raw or steamed in their shells and then the thick skin stripped off the body. Over-demand has led to them becoming rare in the Mediterranean. Similar species are found in Latin America and on the northwest Pacific coast, where they are also farmed.

Squid (alternative name inkfish)

Loliginidae spp.

encornet, calmar (French), *calamar, puntilla* (Spanish), *calamaro* (Italian), *Kalmar,*
Tintenfisch (German), *lula* (Portuguese), *ika* (Japanese)

Unlike cuttlefish, the squid has only a thin bone like a plastic quill inside its soft, oval body. Covered in a speckled purple and black membrane, it has ten arms, two of which are long tentacles, and two fins on either side of its body. It defends itself by firing black ink at any intruder crossing its path and, although giant squid are reputed to live in the dark depths of the Atlantic, most range from 100g (4oz) to 1kg (2¼lb). Different species of squid are distributed throughout the world's oceans.

Octopus
(alternative name devilfish)

Octopus vulgaris

poulpe, pieuvre (live) (French), *pulpo, pop* (Catalan) (Spanish), *polpo, moscardino* (Italian), *Krake, Tintenfisch* (German), *polvo* (Portuguese), *octapodi* (Greek), *tako* (Japanese)

The common octopus is a cold-water dweller but more than 140 other species reside in the world's temperate and tropical seas. The most intelligent of the cephalopod family, an octopus catches its prey by cool appraisal rather than simply diving in. A jelly-like layer of purple-black membrane covers its body, the raw flesh underneath being ivory-coloured and translucent. Its six arms are covered in suction-like tentacles and, unlike squid and cuttlefish, these are its most tender part, having a chewy but smooth texture and full fishy flavour. The major commercial octopus harvesters are Thailand, Korea and the Philippines, an average weight being around 1.5kg (3lb).

Akashi tako

Octopus vulgaris

The Japanese love octopus and none more so than this raspberry-pink beauty that feeds on a rich diet of prawn, plankton and crab. Its food and the fast-moving current of the waters around the town of Akashi have made this *tako* the most highly prized in Japan. Rich in protein, low in fat and high in amino acids, its creamy flesh is soft, velvety and lightly chewy. The Japanese eat it raw – and often still wriggling – as sashimi but it is usually lightly boiled and then thinly sliced and served with cucumber dressed in sweet vinegar or simmered in sweet soy sauce. The meat can also be battered and fried as *akashiyaki*. The traditional way to tenderize it is to knead the flesh in the finely grated pulp of daikon white radish.

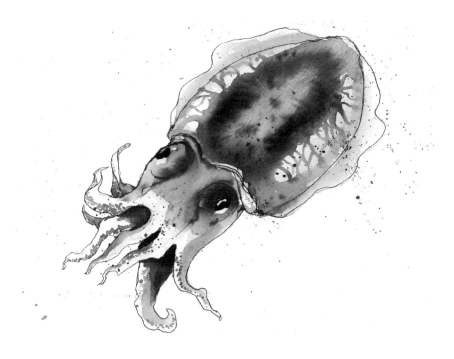

Cuttlefish

Sepia officinalis

seiche (large), casseron (small) (French), *sepia, jibia (large)* (Spanish), *seppia* (Italian),
Sepia, Gemeiner Tintenfisch (German), *choco* (Portuguese)

Similar to squid but it can be tougher. 'Cuttle' refers to its hard white bone, often seen hanging in a budgerigar's cage, that has a spongy interior and can be pumped up by the cuttlefish to give it extra buoyancy. Very messy to prepare, as it contains so much ink, a cuttlefish has ten arms and a glossy, translucent body that darkens from brown to black when handled. Ranging in size from 225–500g (8–18oz), they are at their best when small and young. A tiny related species called *supion*, fried in olive oil and garlic, is a great delicacy in France. Common all over the Mediterranean, off the west coast of Africa, northern Europe and Asia, but not found in North American waters.

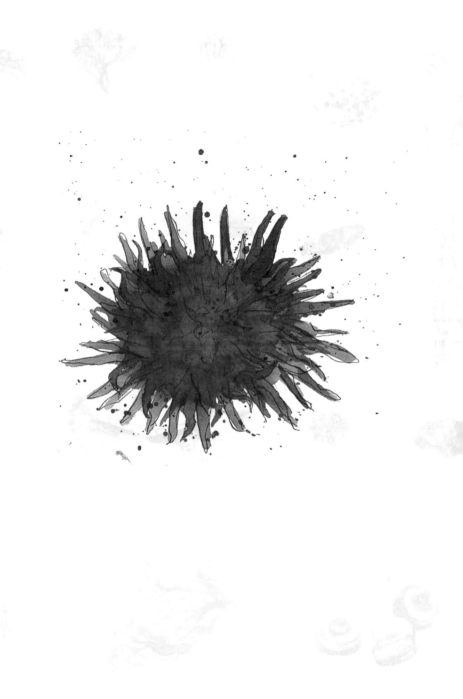

OTHER EDIBLE MARINE LIFE

From the beautiful to the ferocious and ugly to the downright weird, many of the more unusual sea creatures are considered gourmet delicacies in certain parts of the world, often being revered as much as the finest lobster or salmon.

These creatures are not just for the adventurous – some might say reckless – diner, so if you spot a pasta dish of linguine tossed with sea urchin on the menu of a Sicilian trattoria or are offered frogs' legs in a mix of Cajun spices, be brave and give them a try. It could turn out to be a memorable experience – and for all the right reasons!

Sea anemone

Actiniaria

Many varieties of this vividly coloured marine animal, which could be mistaken for an exotic flower, are found in coastal waters around the world. They are carnivorous, feeding off other fish, and spend their time attached to rocks on the seabed or to coral reefs, waiting for prey to swim past to be snared in their venom-filled tendrils. Closely related and similar in texture to jellyfish, two types of sea anemone, the oplet and the beadlet, are eaten in France, where the body cavity is cut into pieces and fried in batter or used in soup.

Violet

Botrylloides violaceus

figue de mer (French), *uovo di mare, limone di mare* (Italian)

Thousands of species of sea squirt can be found around the world firmly attached to rocks and shells in shallow waters but very few cuisines value them as food. Barrel-shaped and looking like a large oyster, the violet projects two siphons, one allowing it to feed by drawing sea water into its body, filtering out plankton and oxygen through a basket-like internal strainer, while the other expels the water out again. In Provence, violets can be served as an expensive addition to a platter of *fruits de mer* or added to a fish stew, although the salty, iodine tang and mushy yellow texture make the flesh, which resembles scrambled egg, an acquired taste. Other varieties are prized in Chile, Korea and Japan, including the sea pineapple, which the Japanese eat raw and has been memorably described in the Lonely Planet guide as 'rubber dipped in ammonia'.

Turtle

Chelonidae

tortue (French), *tortuga* (Spanish), *tartaruga* (Italian), *Schildkrote* (German), *caguama* (Mexico)

Many species of turtle are high on the endangered list and are some of the most protected creatures in the world but others – for example, the softshell turtle in Florida – can still be caught and eaten, and are enjoyed for their lobster- or chicken-like meat. Turtles have four scaly legs and a hard or soft shell and can live on land and in both sea and fresh water. Giant leatherback sea turtles can grow to 2.25m (7½ft) long and weigh over 900kg (2,000lb),

dwarfing freshwater turtles, which are usually smaller, including the North American snapping or green turtle. Previously, turtle soup was an Anglo-American delicacy and it is still eaten in parts of Asia, where turtle meat, skin and innards are all added to a rich herby broth. Soft-shelled turtles are found in fresh water in Europe, Asia, Africa and North and South America, although imported Asian meat may have been illegally sourced.

Sea urchin

Echinus esculentus, Paracentrotus lividus

oursin (French), *erizo de mar* (Spanish), *orsino, riccio di mare* (Italian), *Seeigel* (German),

ourico do mar (Portuguese), *uni* (Japanese)

Around 500 species of this miniature marine hedgehog litter the floors and rocks of the world's seas and woe betide any unsuspecting swimmer who steps on their dagger-like spines. About the size of a small apple, the rounded body has no head or tail but its hard shell contains lobes of roe-like yellow-orange gonads (reproductive organs) that are enjoyed for their intense sweet seaweed flavour. Cuisines across the globe appreciate sea urchins, from the Mediterranean, where they are becoming scarce due to over-consumption, to North America and parts of Asia. In Japan they are considered best eaten raw as sushi and several grades of *uni* are available in the fish markets there, the most sought after being bright, golden and firm. Paler *uni* are considered inferior, being softer and less sweet.

Sea cucumber
(alternative names sea slug, sea rat)

Holothuroidea spp.

beche-de-mer, holthurie (French), *espardenas, espardenyes* (Spanish), *alothuria* (Italian), *Seegurke* (German), *namako* (Japanese), *haishen* (Mandarin), *hoy sum* (Cantonese)

This slug of the deep has no taste but is prized for its texture and ability to absorb other flavours. Different species can be found crawling along the world's seabeds, including 12 off China's coastline, where they are harvested during all but the summer months and also farmed. In China, sea cucumbers are boiled, salted, mixed with ashes and dried in the sun, enabling them to be stored almost indefinitely. Before cooking they are cleaned and rehydrated, and are then simmered for several hours until tender enough to be eaten in stir-fries, chop sueys or a sauce. In Spain, especially around Barcelona, a very different sea cucumber with a squid-like flavour and texture is found. Small, white and tender, it is known as *espardenas* or *espardenyes* and is often grilled with other seafood, Catalan-style.

Lamprey

Petromyzon marinus

lamproie (French), *lamprea* (Spanish), *lampreda* (Italian), *Neunauge, Flussneunauge* (German), *lampreia* (Portuguese)

It might have been around for millions of years but even this primitive creature's mother couldn't honestly say its looks have improved with age. A parasite found in both fresh and salt water, the lamprey survives by clamping itself to other fish and sucking their blood. Its mouth is a circular set of sucking barbs rather than jaws and it has no bones. It can grow to over 90cm (3ft) long and is found off the coasts of France and northern Portugal, as well as in other parts of Europe where over-fishing has made it a protected species. In the US lamprey is fished off the Atlantic and Pacific coasts and from some inland lakes. When caught, a live lamprey has to be bled first and the outer slime scraped off before cooking. The firm-textured flesh is good to eat but is fatty and can be difficult to digest, which could account for the death of the Norman King of England, Henry I who, according to legend, expired in 1135 after dining on 'a surfeit of lampreys'.

Frog

Ranidae

palakang kabaka (Philippines)

Enjoyed since the time of the ancient Chinese dynasties, frog is still highly regarded as a food in China and throughout the Far East where, made into a soup, it is said to reduce fever in the body, detox the system and eliminate excess water. The taste and texture of the black-legged snow frog or Chinese forest frog is similar to chicken. The southern Chinese call it 'chicken of the rice fields', while frogs caught in Thai khlongs are dubbed 'paddy chicken'. In the Philippines the East Asian bullfrog or Taiwanese frog is deep-fried, simmered in vinegar, soy sauce and garlic, or filled with a meat stuffing. In Thailand, buckets of live frogs are a common sight in markets, where they are prepared on the spot and eaten whole in green or red curries.

Frogs' legs

cuisses de grenouille (French), *ancas de rana* (Spanish), *cosce de rana* (Italian), *roschschenkel* (German)

The plump back legs of the common edible frog are a delicacy in both French and Cantonese cuisines but their mild flavour, likened to chicken wings or young farmed rabbit, is also appreciated in the Caribbean, parts of the Mediterranean, and the southern states of the US, in particular Louisiana. In Lyons in France, frogs' legs are cooked with butter, garlic and parsley sauce, in Cajun cuisine they are fried with spices and herbs, and frog leg congee is a signature dish of the Hong Kong Chinese. *Swikee* is a popular frog leg soup in Indonesia, while in Java the skin is fried until crisp and eaten as a snack. Most frogs are harvested as the result of private enterprise so frogs' legs are rarely seen on restaurant menus. They are increasingly being farmed in the US and Asian countries such as Vietnam, despite major animal welfare concerns being raised over international trade in frogs' legs.

Seaweeds

One of the richest sources of vitamins and minerals on earth, seaweed makes an excellent accompaniment to fish and shellfish. With around 5,500 varieties, those most suited to cooking are generally classified in three colour categories – brown varieties, that turn green after cooking, including kombu/konbu, wakame, sea spaghetti and limu kohu; red vareties, inlcuding dulse, carrageen and nori; and green varieties such as sea lettuce.

Brown seaweed

....

Asparagopsis taxiformis

limu kohu (Hawaii)

Of the many varieties of limu seaweed found around Hawaii's coral reefs, limu kohu is the favourite of most islanders. Once gathered, the plants are rinsed, soaked and lightly salted, then pounded and rolled into walnut-size balls for storage. Strongly flavoured, only a little is needed to season stews, salads and the local sashimi dishes known as *poke*.

Carrageen

....

Chondrus crispus

Often called Irish moss, carrageen is prolific around the coastlines of Europe and North America. Rich and dark red when fresh, once dried in the open air it bleaches to a creamy colour. Well known for its

gelatinous properties, it can be used as a vegetarian alternative to gelatin in jellies and other set dishes. In China, a related algae called black hair moss is found on land rather than in water. Sold dried, it can be added to stir-fries and other dishes after being soaked and rinsed in fresh water.

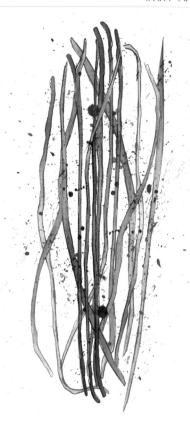

Sea spaghetti

Himanthalia elongata

Long, almost flat and spaghetti-like, this Atlantic seaweed is also known as 'sea thong'. Pan-fried briefly with garlic and pepper it makes a good side dish for fish and shellfish, particularly scallops.

Water convolvulus
(*alternative names water spinach, swamp cabbage*)

Ipomoea aquatica
kangkung (Indonesia), *pak boong* (Thai), *rau muong* (Vietnamese)

A tall green plant with long hollow stems that flourishes in waterways throughout East and Southeast Asia. Introduced into the US several years ago, its prolific growth rate has turned it into an unwelcome weed in some states, particularly Florida and Texas. An important vegetable in Malay and Chinese cuisines, it is added to stir-fries, cooked with cuttlefish in a sweet and spicy sauce, and can also be eaten raw such as in a Lao green papaya salad.

Kombu/konbu

Laminaria japonica

Also known as Neptune's belt, dashima (Korea), haidal (China), or kelp, this Japanese seaweed is widely eaten in East Asia. Around 90 per cent of the market product is cultivated and harvested in Hokkaido and it is one of the three main ingredients in dashi soup stock. Thick and glossy black-green in colour, the large fresh kombu leaves should only be wiped with paper towels before use so the surface flavour is not lost. Kombu should be removed just before a liquid comes to a boil to prevent it imparting a bitter taste.

Nori

Porphyra miniata

Although classified as a red seaweed, nori turns
black or green when dry and can be lightly grilled or
toasted on one side over a high heat to make it crisp.
Ready-toasted sheets of yaki-nori seaweed are sold
in packages in Japanese food stores and are used
for wrapping rolled sushi or crumbling over steamed
rice. In Wales, nori is known as laver or purple laver,
and is boiled and then pureed to make the famous
laver bread. Traditionally eaten with bacon and
cockles for breakfast, it can also be served as a soup
or a sauce to accompany lamb, fish and shellfish.

Dulse

Rhodymenia palmata

Also known as sea parsley, this has a slightly
crunchy, nutty taste and is very popular in Ireland,
where it is known as dillisk. It can be served raw in a
salad, added to a stir-fry or included in a fish pie.

Samphire
(alternative name sea asparagus)
Salicornia europaea

Two types of samphire – rock and marsh – are found
in estuaries, rocky pools and marshlands along the
coastlines of northern France and the British Isles.
Related to parsley and fennel, samphire has small
green branches with tips but no leaves and looks very
like its alternative name of sea asparagus. Blanching
or steaming removes some of its salty flavour, leaving
a fresh, pleasantly crunchy green vegetable that
makes a great accompaniment to fish dishes. Fresh
samphire is best between May and September, after
which it can be too woody. It is also pickled, which is
available all year round.

Water chestnut
Trapa natans
biqi (Mandarin), *mati* (Cantonese)

The Cantonese name means 'horse's hoof', due to
its shape and brown skin, but the Chinese water
chestnut is not a nut but the rhizome of a bush
cultivated in rice fields across China. The newly dug
chestnuts are first washed to remove mud and then
peeled to reveal the snow-white vegetable inside,
which has a crunchy, juicy texture and mildly sweet
taste. As fresh water chestnuts spoil quickly, most
are sold canned and need to be sliced, cut into
julienne or chopped before being added to a stir-fry
or salad. In China, street stalls sell fresh unpeeled
water chestnuts caramelised and threaded onto
bamboo skewers and, in summer, skewers of whole
raw chestnuts as a refreshing snack.

Sea lettuce

Ulva lactuca

Sometimes known as green laver, this popular seaweed has a taste similar to sorrel. Widely distributed among the world's oceans, including off the coasts of the British Isles, Scandinavia, China and Japan, its broad leaves can be added to salads and soups, wrapped around fish to be steamed or deep-fried for genuine crispy seaweed.

Wakame

Undaria pinnatifida

Used in Japanese miso soup, this is bright green and leafy, has a briny, oyster-like flavour, and is the best seaweed for serving as a vegetable and in salads. Native to East Asia, it has spread to other countries, notably New Zealand, where it has become a seriously invasive algae. Sold dried or salted, wakame needs to be cut into small pieces because it expands during cooking.

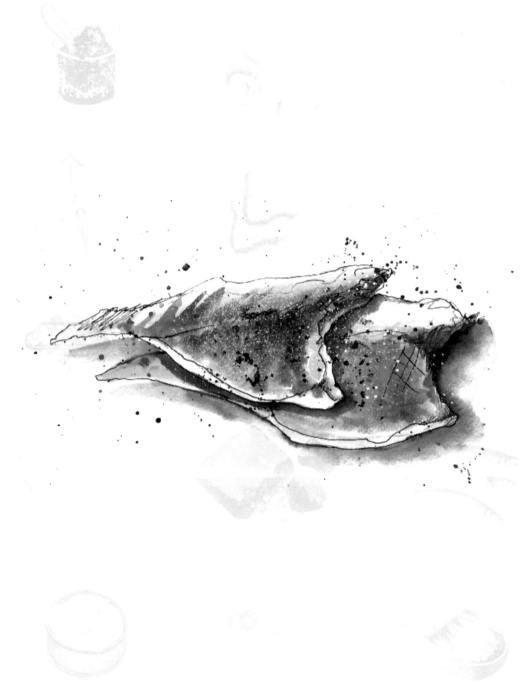

PRESERVED FISH

Once the first refrigerator had been invented in the late 19th century, the necessity to dry, smoke, salt or pickle fish to ensure a year-round supply gradually disappeared but, old habits die hard, and down the centuries people had developed a taste for their particular way of preserving fish and kept their traditional methods alive.

Today, preserved fish plays a popular part in many cuisines. In the US, a bagel just wouldn't be the same without a generous topping of lox and soured cream. A crisp wafer of Bombay duck adds the finishing touch to an Indian curry and no Cockney celebration in London's East End is complete without a tub of jellied eels.

Smoked fish

Many different species of fish are smoked, from white fish such as cod, whiting and halibut to oil-rich species like salmon, mackerel, trout, herring, bluefish and tuna. Fish can either be cold- or hot-smoked.

Cold-smoked fish

Cold smoked fish come in two styles: fully cured and partially cured.

Full curing is used for many types of fish including halibut, sturgeon, tuna, swordfish and marlin but, most famously, salmon. The freshly caught fish are filleted and then either coated in dry salt or soaked in brine. The length of salting time ranges from a few minutes to many hours, depending on the size and thickness of the fish, and draws much of the moisture out of the flesh but also allows a little salt to soak into it. The excess salt is then washed off before the fish is cured a second time.

The recipes for individual cures are kept as closely guarded secrets by the smokehouses but can include sugar, spices, rum, whisky, heather and even beetroot. The cured fish is hung up and smoked for 12 to 24 hours or longer over wood shavings (usually oak, beech or alder), the temperature never rising high enough to cook the fish, so it retains the smooth, melt-in-the-mouth texture of the finest raw fish. Served in wafer-thin slices, it has a rich, pleasantly oily flavour.

Partially cured cold-smoked fish such as Finnan haddie, Glasgow pale, hilsa and herring (kipper and bloater) must be cooked before eating.

Salmon
(alternative names lox, nova)

The most celebrated of all cold-smoked fish, modern methods for smoking salmon are based on those first developed in Tsarist Russia. In the late 19th century, Russian pogroms forced many Jews to escape; they emigrated and settled on the edge of

cities like London and New York and begin smoking salmon, one of their favourite foods from home. Also known as lox, particularly in Canada and on the east coast of the US, after the German word *Lachs* meaning salmon, another alternative name is nova, which dates from the days when much of the smoked salmon eaten in New York came from Nova Scotia. Smoked salmon is traditionally served in thin slices with chopped hard-cooked egg, capers and finely chopped shallot with lemon juice squeezed over, or piled into bagels on a thick bed of cream cheese.

Trout

Similar to smoked salmon, but with a lighter, more delicate flavour.

Sturgeon

A great favourite with not only the Russian tsars but many other European royals too, smoked sturgeon is prized as the finest of smoked fish. King Edward II of England declared it a royal fish, presumably because he wanted to keep it all for himself! The thin, creamy slices are edged with deep gold and have an incomparable flavour. Hot-smoked sturgeon is also available.

Halibut

The translucent snow-white slices of smoked halibut are tinged with gold along the edge. They have a light smoky flavour and are excellent as part of a smoked fish platter.

Finnan haddie

Records of smoked fish in Scotland date from the 16th century, but early methods involved heavy smoking to preserve the fish, which consequently became tough to eat. In the late 19th century the village of Findon (pronounced 'Finnan') refined the process by lightly smoking haddock, giving it a more delicate flavour and finer texture. Finnan haddie is best served grilled and topped with butter. A similar Scottish smoked haddock is Glasgow pale.

Kipper

A smoked herring that is popular in the British Isles, where it is often served as a hearty breakfast. The whole herring is split from tail to head, opened out, and then salted and smoked. The name 'kipper' is believed to derive either from *kippa*, the Icelandic word for 'pull' or 'snatch', or the English word 'kipe', referring to a basket used to catch fish. First produced by John Woodger, a fish smoker from Seahouses, Northumberland, in the 1840s; today some of the finest kippers come from the Isle of Man.

Bloater

A bloater is an ungutted herring that has been smoked whole.

Hilsa

ilish, elish (Bengali)

Fish is a staple part of Bengali cuisine but hilsa is the most highly prized. A bony, oily, silver-skinned fish, it migrates in late February from the Bay of Bengal, traveling inland to lay its eggs in rivers across India. The national fish of Bangladesh (East Bengal), it is also popular in West Bengal, especially the capital Kolkata, where smoked hilsa is regarded as the finest way to eat it. Often spread with a spice mix of ground mustard seeds, salt, mustard oil and turmeric, the hilsa is wrapped in banana leaves and cooked with rice. Extremely sweet and juicy, smoked hilsa has a delicate texture and aroma, and due to its boniness is usually served filleted.

Hot-smoked fish

Hot-smoked fish is prepared in the same way as cold-smoked, but the fish is cooked during the smoking process as the temperature of the smoke is gradually increased. Hot-smoking takes less time than cold so the flesh remains flaky and moist and doesn't dry out by overcooking. Hot-smoked fish cannot be sliced but breaks into firm, thick flakes.

Some shellfish is also hot-smoked such as oysters, mussels and langoustines.

Arbroath smokie

The most highly regarded hot-smoked haddock are the 'smokies' from the town of Abroath on the east coast of Scotland where, since the early 19th century, haddock have been smoked whole in pairs. Known colloquially as 'pinwiddies', the gutted fish are dry-salted for two hours then tied in pairs and hung over wooden rods. After washing to remove the salt, they are then smoked over oak or beech. The best way to enjoy the melting, flaky flesh of an Arbroath smokie is 'hot off the barrel', still warm from the smoking process.

Buckling

A hot-smoked herring that has its head and guts removed but its roe left in. Can be eaten hot or cold.

Red herring

A whole, ungutted herring with a strong, distinctive flavour. It is salted for a month and then smoked for a week, the smoking process turning it bright red.

Mackerel

A popular and versatile fish, smoked mackerel has a juicy, rounded, almost buttery flavour, balanced by a light smokiness. Peel away the glossy skin and add the flaked flesh to a salad, kedgeree or risotto, or mash with sour cream to make a pâté.

Snoek
A South African speciality, snoek is a cousin of the mackerel, found in the temperate waters of the southern hemisphere. In its fresh state it is cooked in many different ways, but when smoked it makes an excellent fish pâté, or it can be flaked with tomatoes and peppers for a kedgeree-style dish called *smoorsnoek* (another word). Salty and with a good texture due to partial drying and smoking, smoked snoek flakes off its many sharp bones quite easily.

Salmon
(alternative name kippered salmon)

Very different from the translucent slices of cold-smoked salmon, hot-smoked breaks into large flakes like fresh salmon, has a more concentrated oily flavour, and turns dark red on the outside while the inner flesh remains pink. The American Indians of the Pacific northwest coast traditionally prepare hard-smoked salmon (or salmon jerky), where the fish is cured with salt, sugar and spices and then smoked until hard.

Trout

Different flavour strengths of smoked trout are available, depending on the hardwood used as smoking chips. Strongly flavoured oak and the milder beech are both common in the UK, hickory is popular in the US, whereas in parts of eastern and northern Europe juniper is preferred. The increase in farmed rainbow trout has led to improved quality and wider availability. The natural partner for the firm, lightly flavoured flesh is creamed horseradish.

Eel

gerookte paling (Dutch)

Originally eaten by the Maori people of New Zealand, smoked eel's popularity has spread around the world and it is considered a particular delicacy in the Netherlands. The Dutch peel away the shiny, golden skin to reveal firm, compact flesh, which is pulled directly off the bones and eaten as a snack. Smoky, rich and oily, smoked eel is especially good with creamed horseradish.

Sprat
(alternative name brisling)

kilud (Estonian)

The best smoked sprats are considered to be those that hale from the Baltic capitals of Tallinn and Riga. The small fish, smoked to a pale gold, have a deliciously sweet, slightly spicy flavour. Being too small to fillet, the whole fish is eaten, including the bones, tail and head, which give the soft flesh a pleasantly crunchy texture.

Dried, salted and cured fish
(and other marine life)

Although modern technology and refrigeration have done away with the need to salt food in order to preserve it, salting fish actually changes its flavour and texture, giving it a stronger taste and making it firmer, meaning that products such as salt cod are still highly prized today.

Gravlax
(alternative name gravad lax)

gravlaks (Norway and Denmark)

In the past, salmon was an important food for Scandinavians and to preserve the large quantities that arrived during the spring spawning season, the fish were fermented using a small amount of salt and then buried in a hole, or *grav* (grave), in the ground. In Sweden, this preservation process became a commercial enterprise in the 1300s, continuing until the 17th century when it grew closer to the sweet cure using dill, sugar and salt that we know today. To preserve stocks of wild salmon, most fish for gravlax is now farmed.

Served sliced thinly like smoked salmon, the slices are edged with a distinctive border of the chopped fresh dill that coated the whole fillet. The soft flesh melts in the mouth and has a sweet, herby flavour. The traditional accompaniment to gravlax is a sharply flavoured cold sauce of mustard and dill, rather than lemon juice.

Mosciame del tonno

An Italian speciality made by salting, curing and
sun-drying strips of tuna, following ancient methods
that date back to Phoenician and Roman times.
Thought to have originated in Liguria, mosciame is
now associated with Carloforte, a small island off the
south of Sardinia, where Ligurian fishermen settled
in the 1700s. Drying the tuna in the salty, coastal
breezes of the Mediterranean turns the flesh a rich,
red-brown colour and imparts an extra depth to its
flavour, making it similar to a cured ham but with
subtle fishy overtones.

The tuna loins are first cleaned and then cured
with sea salt, before being rinsed and hung up to
dry. Mosciame is served cut into wafer-thin slices,
drizzled with extra-virgin olive oil, and lemon juice
squeezed over, or grated into pastas or salads.

In Spain, tuna cured and dried in the same way
is called *mojama* and in Portugal it is known
as *mochama*.

Salt cod

morue (French), *bacalao* (Spanish), *baccala* (Italian),
bacalhau (Portuguese)

Huge flat slabs of salt cod might look unappetizing –
and smell even worse – on the fishmonger's counter,
but after being soaked for between 24 and 48 hours
the fish develops a firm, moist, flaky texture and
has a stronger flavour than it did in its fresh state.
Salt cod has been produced in Canada, Iceland and
Norway for over 500 years and it is very popular in
Mediterranean countries where it is made into fritters
and fried in batter or pounded with garlic and olive
oil to make *brandade de morue*. Diminishing stocks
of North Atlantic cod have brought about the arrival
of salted Pacific cod, and other species such as ling,
haddock and pollock are used. Originally dried
naturally on racks by the wind and sun, most salt cod
is now dried indoors using electric heaters.

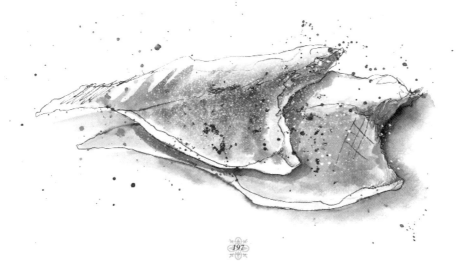

Salt herring

By the 12th century, the herring was a staple part of the European diet and salting was a reliable way of preserving the prolific catches. The traditional way of doing this – still used in Norway, the Netherlands and the British Isles, in particular in the Orkney islands and the Isle of Man – involves layering the fish with coarse salt in barrels and leaving them with a weight on top for up to four days. The herrings then need to be soaked in several changes of fresh water for up to two days to remove the salt before they can be eaten raw, dressed with oil and lemon juice, sour cream, or onion rings, and accompanied by bread or boiled potatoes. They can also be baked, grilled or added to pies.

Stockfish

stockfish (French), *stoccafisso* (Italian), *Stockfisch* (German), *peixe seco* (Portuguese), *stokkfisk, klippfisk* (Norwegian), *stokvis* (Dutch)

The name given to unsalted fish, especially cod, that has been dried in the sun and wind on wooden racks, the cool, breezy northern climes of Iceland and Lofoten in Norway being particularly suited to this. Stockfish is widely eaten in Mediterranean countries such as Italy, Spain and Portugal, and it is a staple part of Caribbean cooking, having been taken to the West Indies on slave ships. It was also important in the diets of the early British settlers in New England and Nova Scotia.

Lutefisk
(alternative name lutfisk)

Made from air-dried stockfish, usually cod, but ling, haddock and pollock may also be used, lutefisk is eaten in Scandinavian countries, Canada and the US from November through to Christmas. The stockfish is first soaked in several changes of cold water for five to six days, then transferred to a soaking solution of water and caustic lye soda for two days, so the fish swells to a larger size than it was in its original state and develops a gelatinous texture. The soaked fish has to be cooked carefully to prevent it collapsing, which is usually done by gentle steaming or baking in the oven in a covered container. Lutefisk made from cod smells quite strongly, other species less so, and all have mild-flavoured flesh. The Scandinavians attribute their long, healthy lives to eating lutefisk.

Hakarl

The Greenland shark inhabits Iceland's chilly waters and, although toxic when eaten fresh, the Inuit taught the local population how it could be used for food. The Inuit discovered that if buried in the frosty ground all winter, the poison in the shark melted away. The process was refined so that now the meat is first buried and then hung up to dry. Icelanders might love it, but the lack of foreign takers says it all.

Chinese salted fish

yan yu, xian yu (Chinese)

The Chinese preserve both marine and freshwater fish with salt using three basic methods. The first is to clean the fish, layer it with salt and press it for 10 days to extract excess liquid before washing away the salt and drying the fish. The other methods involve preserving the fish in brine before drying or simply drying it with or without salt, depending on the type of fish. It is often used to boost the flavour of bland foods such as rice or added to stews and soups.

Conpoy
(dried scallops)

Atrina pectinata, Pationopecten yessoensis

ganbel (Chinese)

Made from scallops gathered off China's north coast in April, July and August, conpoy is made by sun-drying the cooked scallop meat. Strongly flavoured and very expensive, it needs to be soaked before being cooked. Ground conpoy is traditionally sprinkled as a garnish over crisp seaweed but most restaurants substitute a cheaper mix of ground fried fish instead.

Shark's fin

....

yuchi (Chinese)

Shark has been a popular delicacy in China since the Tang dynasty (618–907) when it was first made into a relish. Seven or eight species of shark are fished off China's coastline and the fins from the belly, back and tail are all processed for culinary use. Although shark's fin is extremely nutritious – it contains calcium and phosphorus and hardly any fat – this is not the reason the Chinese prize it, nor is it for its flavour, which is negligible. Shark's fin's popularity lies in its rarity and the prestige it affords a special banquet such as for a wedding. The fins, usually from mako, blue or hammerhead sharks, are cured during spring and summer, soaked in fresh water to remove the blood and dried in the sun.

Dried shark's fin is available from Asian food stores. It is very expensive and preparing it for cooking is a laborious task. The dried fin must first be soaked in cold water for three days to soften it, then simmered for several hours – changing the cooking water regularly – until the outer skin comes away easily and the bone can be removed. When the fin becomes transparent and curls, it is rinsed and then cooked for about an hour with other ingredients such as meat, poultry, vegetables and spices to add a crunchy, glutinous texture to a stew or soup.

Conservation agencies cite the collection of shark's fin as a cause of the rapid decline in the world's shark population, and the fins are said to contain high levels of mercury. Fake shark's fin is produced from mung bean pasta.

Dried abalone

....

pao yu (Chinese)

As with shark's fin, abalone is a symbol of prestige and wealth in China. Available fresh and canned, it can also be bought sun-dried which extends its shelf life to a year. Dried abalone should have no cracks or mould, nor be very dark in colour. Time-consuming to prepare, it needs to be soaked and then simmered for several hours to soften it. Once cooked, dried abalone adds a concentrated rich, savoury flavour to dishes and can be served whole or sliced, and added to soups or stir-fried with oyster sauce.

Dried prawns

....

udang sirin (Malaysian), *xiagan, xiami* (Chinese)

Important in Chinese and other Asian cuisines, sun-dried prawns are sold both whole and peeled. Large, medium and small prawns are dried, although the largest measure no more than 1.25cm (½in) and the smallest have to be left whole because they are too tiny to peel. Also called sea rice, as only salt-water prawns are dried, after soaking they can be added to

salads, soups, stews and noodle dishes and are also
used as one of the 'eight-treasure' stuffing ingredients
for duck.

Dried anchovy

kozhuva (Kerala and south India), *ikan bilis, setipinna taty*
(Malaysian), *ikan teri* (Indonesia)

Prepared and served in the same way as dried
prawns in Southeast Asian countries.

Dried squid

Sun-dried squid has a chewy texture and strong
smell, and in China it is valued for the distinctive
flavour it gives to dishes. First soaked overnight to
soften the flesh, it can be added to soups, stir-fries
and stews. In the Philippines, the soaking stage is
omitted and dried whole squid are grilled or fried
in vegetable oil to produce one of the most pungent-
smelling delicacies on offer in the food markets of
Manila and other towns and cities. Bags of dried
shredded squid are a popular snack served with
drinks in many Asian countries, including Japan,
Taiwan, Vietnam, Macau, Hong Kong and Korea.

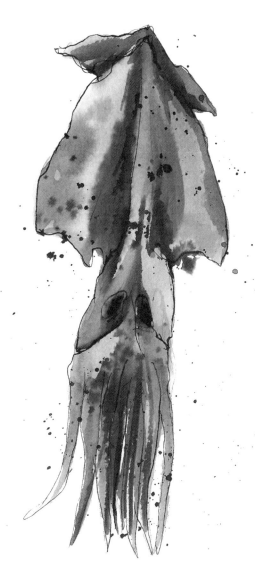

Bombay duck
Harpadon nehereus

Brittle in texture and crumbly in the mouth, with an anchovy-like tang, Bombay duck is something you either love or hate. Produced from the bummalow, a fish living in Asian waters, especially the estuaries and coastal areas around Mumbai. In India the fish is sometimes served fresh but more often it is filleted, salted and dried in the sun where it develops a powerful smell. One – probably apocryphal – story attributes its name to the days of the Raj, when fish being transported by train made the carriages smell so bad, the British christened the odor 'Bombay dak', after the train. To prepare, fry the Bombay duck for a few minutes and serve hot with curries.

Bonito flakes
hana-katsuo, katsuobushi (Japanese)

Produced in Japan by steaming, drying, smoking and curing fresh bonito until it becomes hard enough to be shaved into flakes, a process that takes six months. The shaved flakes are an essential ingredient in the Japanese soup stock, dashi.

Fish maw
yudu (Chinese)

A Chinese delicacy that's probably not to the taste of most Western palates, fish maw is the air bladder of certain fish, mainly two different species of croaker. It is sun-dried for a week and then deep-fried. Looking like a giant prawn cracker, it needs to be soaked for around 30 minutes before being added to soups, stews or a traditional Mongolian fire pot, where – like a fondue – each diner cooks their own

selection of meat, vegetables and fish by dropping the pieces into a bubbling pot of stock, which at the end of the meal is eaten as a soup.

Gulbi

A Korean delicacy made from dried, salted yellow croaker, said to act as a tonic. The fish must be very fresh and needs to be caught carefully to avoid any surface damage that could impair its quality. Sun- and wind-dried, the croaker are salted with natural salt that has been previously stored for a year. Full-flavoured and rich, the salted roe is also eaten.

Shisamo
Spinrinchus lanceolatus

A small, marine fish, known as capelin in Canada. It is about 10–15cm (4–6 in) long and has an olive back, shading to silver on the sides. Common to the northern Pacific and the Atlantic Oceans, the fish move into fresh water to spawn and are caught in large numbers at the mouth of Japan's Kushiro river when they swim upstream in October and November. The females are full of roe, which is highly prized and during the fall served in local restaurants as sushi and sashimi.

Most shisamo, however, are salted, sun-dried and threaded onto long bamboo skewers with their mouths gaping open, to be grilled in open-air food markets. The salting and sun-drying not only preserve the fish but break down protein to create amino acids which produce *umami*, the fifth 'savoury' basic taste after salt, sour, sweet and bitter. Grilled shisamo are chewy and meaty and impart all five of these basic flavours.

Prawn crackers
(alternative name shrimp chips)

krupuk (Indonesia), *xiapian* (Chinese),
bahn phong tom (Vietnamese)

These addictive pre-dinner nibbles are made by
blending fresh prawns with a starch, such as tapioca
flour, and salt and sugar. The grey, translucent discs
look distinctly unappetizing in their raw state, but
as soon as they hit the hot oil, they puff up and curl
into crisp, pinky white crackers.

Jellyfish

dikya (Philippines), *kurage* (Japanese), *ubor-ubor*
(Malaysian), *haizhe* (Chinese), *hoy cheek* (Cantonese),
sua (Vietnamese)

Not a fish at all but a marine invertebrate, jellyfish
is never eaten fresh from the sea but is always
sold either dried in large round discs formed from
the umbrella-shaped body, or rehydrated. Almost
transparent, with soft trailing tentacles and a head
similar to a cuttlefish or squid, the body is separated
from the head and stinging tentacles which are
discarded. The body is then cleaned, soaked, salted
with baking soda and dried. Dried jellyfish needs
soaking overnight in several changes of water to rid
it of excess salt, after which it is cut into strips and
blanched, which makes the strips curl.

Entirely tasteless, jellyfish is eaten purely for its
unique texture that has been described as 'tender,
crunchy and elastic' or, more prosaically, as 'elastic
bands'. Served on platters at Chinese banquets
dressed with soy sauce, rice vinegar, sesame oil and
mustard, it resembles a heap of translucent golden
noodles. In Japan it is an ingredient in the seafood
and vegetable salad *sunomono*.

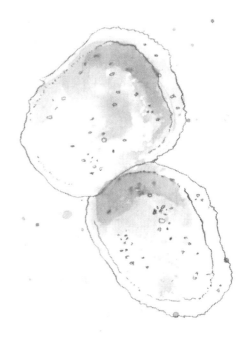

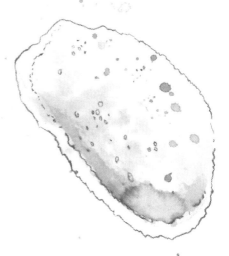

Dried and salted roe

Caviar

ikra (Russian), *khag-avar* (Persian)

Beluga, the finest caviar, demands a king's ransom as the price to be paid for enjoying this lightly salted roe of the female sturgeon. Living in the Caspian and Black Seas, the beluga sturgeon is the largest, oldest and rarest of the species and takes 20 years to reach maturity, hence the high price commanded for its roe. Pale to dark steely grey in colour, with a soft creamy texture and delicate nutty flavour, the smooth beluga eggs seem to 'pop' as they burst in the mouth and are larger than the eggs of sevruga and oscietra caviars that come from other sturgeon species. All three species have been severely over-fished in the Black Sea, and sturgeon in the Caspian Sea is now protected.

Traditionally served in a small glass or china dish set in crushed ice, caviar is accompanied by blinis, sour cream and a shot or three of pure Russian vodka. It should be served with a special spoon made of bone as metal would taint the flavour of the precious eggs.

Caviar d'Aquitaine

As Russian and Iranian caviar has declined and become a luxury only to be enjoyed by the few, a sustainable alternative is now being successfully farmed in Aquitaine, southwest France. During the first half of the 20th century, the roe of wild sturgeon caught in the Gironde estuary became popular as caviar but over-fishing and destruction of habitat brought stocks to the brink of extinction. Today the Siberian baeri sturgeon thrives in the warm waters of Aquitaine's fish farms, reaching maturity in seven to 10 years, whereas in Siberia it would take double that time. Male fish are sold as wet fish fillets after three or four years, while the females are nurtured until their eggs are considered to be of a sufficient size and quality. The dark grey eggs have a light, almost smoky flavour, and release a pale, creamy oil when pressed. Caviar is also farmed in other parts of Europe, including Latvia and Italy.

Paddlefish caviar

A cartilaginous relative of the sturgeon, the grey paddlefish or spoonbill is native to North America, where only roe from sturgeon and paddlefish can be termed 'caviar'. Found in the Mississippi and Tennessee rivers, the roe is harvested under controlled conditions to protect stocks. The small, silver-grey or gold eggs have a buttery and mild flavour with a soft texture. Also known as *malossol*, meaning 'less salt', in Russian, this refers to the way the eggs are processed.

Other caviar is harvested from the hackleback sturgeon, a fast-growing native of the Mississippi and Missouri rivers; also the white sturgeon, which is farm-raised in California; and the highly prized lake sturgeon from Canada.

Lumpfish roe
(alternative name lumpsucker roe)

The lumpfish was largely dismissed as bycatch only fit for dog or cat food until the possibilities of marketing its roe as a caviar alternative were realised. A bottom-dweller that lays its eggs in shallow waters, the unlovely lumpfish with its big head and piggy eyes was historically eaten by Scandinavians who enjoyed its oily flesh but appreciated by few others. The untreated eggs from a mature female can be any colour of the rainbow but after salting and processing they are dyed either red or black. Pleasantly fishy, the small eggs can be used as a garnish or as a topping for small crackers for a pre-dinner nibble.

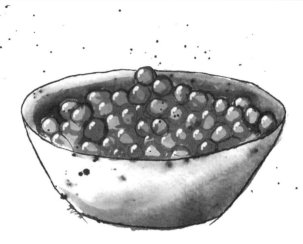

Arënkha ®

Although it looks like roe, Arënkha is actually made in the Netherlands from smoked herring fillet that is transformed into tiny, glossy pearls by a unique process similar to the molecular gastronomy pioneered at El Bulli Restaurant in Spain. A viable and more ethical alternative to caviar, it's similar in taste to the real thing but costs only a fraction of the price. Avruga is similar but made from herring roe.

Kazunoko

Traditionally eaten in Japan on New Year's Eve, the name of this salted herring roe translates as 'many children', and is a symbol of fertility and prosperity. The tiny, crunchy yellow roe is harvested from the fish or scooped off kombu (a type of seaweed, see page 184) where the herring lays its eggs. The roe, known as 'yellow diamonds' in Japan, has to be soaked for a day before it can be served in sake, mirin and soy sauce and sprinkled with bonito flakes. It has a salty flavour with a touch of bitterness.

Keta salmon roe

ikura (Japanese)

The roe of the red (chum) salmon takes its name of 'keta' from the Russian word for that fish. The large eggs are golden orange in colour, have the sweet, honeyed taste and oiliness of fresh salmon and are used for sushi and as a garnish for fish dishes and scrambled eggs. *Sujiko* is Japanese salmon roe sold still in its membrane. Darker red than keta roe, it has a stronger flavour and is used for sushi and sashimi.

Poutargue

A Provençal speciality from Martigues in the Bouches du Rhône, poutargue is the dried roe of grey mullet. The egg pouches are carefully removed intact from the fish, covered in coarse salt and left for six to eight hours, before being rinsed and then pressed between two planks of wood to flatten them. After being air-dried for three to six days, they are covered in wax to extend their life. Before serving, the wax is removed and the roe cut into very thin slices or grated over hunks of country bread. Poutargue has a delicate briny, but not over fishy, flavour.

Bottarga di Muggine is similar to poutargue but it can also be made from tuna roe. The best bottarga comes from grey mullet fished from the salty waters of Lake Cabras in western Sardinia.

Tarama

The salted, cured roe of grey mullet or carp were originally used for making the Greek mezze, *taramasalata*, but as stocks of both fish declined, cod roe has largely taken their place. There are two types of tarama: white, which is considered the best, and pink, which is dyed. To make *taramasalata*, the roe is pounded with olive oil, lemon, a little chopped onion and either breadcrumbs or mashed potato, to make it go further and soften its strong flavour. It was traditionally a fasting food for Lent as it contains no meat or dairy products.

Wasabi tobiko

The processed eggs of flying fish, wasabi tobiko is becoming increasingly popular outside Japan for its striking emerald colour and spicy kick of Japanese horseradish. Other tobikos are flavoured with jalapeno and are dark green in colour, or they can be tinted with squid ink and black. A popular topping for sushi, the roe of farmed capelin (a small Arctic fish resembling smelt) from Iceland and Denmark can sometimes be passed off as tobiko. Hard and crunchy, the tiny loose eggs burst in the mouth but, beyond the wasabi 'hit', have little flavour.

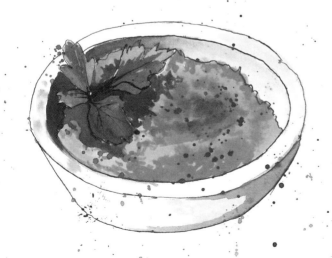

Crab roe

Used in Asia as a gourmet garnish for steamed dumplings and seafood dishes, added to soups and sauces or simply scooped out of the cooked shell and enjoyed on its own, crab roe is rich, sweet and briny.

The Shanghai hairy crab provides an abundant supply of sticky orange roe, as does Hong Kong's yellow oil crab, while in other parts of Southeast Asia large mud crabs are the most common source. One dish from southern China involves curing the raw mud crab's roe by steeping it in soy sauce and spices for two days, which transforms it into a vivid red paste.

In the Philippines, *taba ng talangka* is made from the roe of small crabs, which is then cooked with garlic and the juice of calamansi limes and eaten with rice. In America's Deep South, crab roe is often used to make she-crab soup, a cross between a chowder and a bisque.

Jellied eels

An iconic English delicacy, long enjoyed by the cockneys of London's East End, where pie and mash shops and jellied eel stalls can still be found among the curry houses in Brick Lane and the surrounding area. Eaten as a street food rather than being prepared at home, the popularity of jellied eels possibly dates from the time of the Huguenots who, crossing the Channel to escape persecution in their native France and settling on the edge of the City of London, may have introduced their traditional recipe for *aspic d'anguille* into their new surroundings.

Before pollution forced them to close, eel fisheries were well established along the Thames and although eels are now returning to the river, most used for jellied eels these days come from Lough Neagh in Northern Ireland. The eels are cut into 2.5–5cm (1–2 in) pieces and cooked in a vegetable stock, with lemon and nutmeg often added; because the fish are fatty the cooking liquid becomes jellied as it cools.

Rollmops

The name of these sweet and sour herring fillets comes from the German word *rollen*, meaning 'to roll'. The unskinned fillets are first marinated, then rolled around a pearl onion or gherkin and secured with a toothpick. Popular in many north European countries, including Germany, Scandinavia, the Czech Republic, Slovakia and parts of the British Isles, the marinade mix varies from country to country but generally includes white vinegar, water, onion rings, mustard seeds, whole peppercorns, sugar and salt. Soft, with a shiny appearance and melting texture, rollmops have a sweet–sour flavour and are excellent with dark rye and sourdough breads.

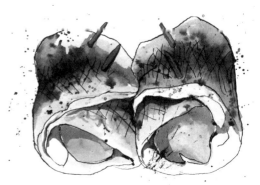

Soused herring

A cooked herring that is marinated in vinegar and other flavourings, 'soused' means something that has been soaked in a mild preserving liquid. The herring can be baked or fried in the marinade, to which bay leaves, sugar, mace and chopped onion are added, and then left to soak in it until cold. Cider, wine and tea are also sometimes used instead of vinegar. In Germany, *Bratheringe* are herring that have been floured, fried and steeped in vinegar for 24 hours.

Surströmming

A traditional Swedish delicacy with a sweet–salty taste mellowing to a well-matured cheesiness on the palate, that is only for the brave. Its name, which means 'sour herring', and the pungent, all-pervasive smell of rotten eggs and worse that it gives off, are guaranteed to deter all but its most devoted fans. In north Sweden each year the appearance of surströmming on the third Thursday in August gives rise to great celebrations and even greater consumption. Made for centuries from fermented herring, which was an alternative way of preserving the fish without curing it with salt or smoke, today most is produced on the island of Ulvon. More then a million cans are produced each year with more and more being exported to countries such as Japan, well known for its love of robust culinary sensations. Surströmming is eaten with almond potatoes, chopped onion and a flatbread known as *tunnbrod*.

Canned, bottled and preserved fish

Canned fish

When Napoleon offered a huge reward to anyone who could invent a method of preserving food to keep his great army on the move, a Frenchman called Nicolas Appert came up with the idea of sterilizing food in jars. During the 1800s, inventors replaced the jars with cans, which led to the first canning factory being built in New York City in 1812.

Fish are canned immediately after being caught to ensure their nutrients and eating quality are retained. Canned fish contain more calcium than fresh fish as the process softens small bones in the flesh so they can be eaten as well. Fish are usually canned in oil (olive or sunflower), brine or sea water but they can also be in tomato sauce or other savoury dressings.

Canned salmon, mackerel, sardines, anchovies and kippers are all good sources of omega-3 fatty acids. Tuna, canned in brine or sea water, is lower in fat than fresh tuna as the canning process removes the fat. Shellfish such as prawns, crab meat, clams, mussels and oysters are also canned, often in brine.

Asian fish sauce

An important and distinctive ingredient in Thai, Vietnamese and Filipino cooking made from salted, fermented fish or prawns. Rich in protein and B vitamins, it is used in marinades, dressings and dipping sauces. The best-quality fish sauce is a rich golden brown colour and has a salty, pungent flavour. Known as *nam pla* in Thailand, *nuoc mam* in Vietnam, and *patis* in the Philippines, it is frequently used in these countries in much the same way as soy sauce is used in China. Chinese prawn sauce has a similar flavour but is not quite as salty.

Colatura di Alici

Similar to Asian fish sauce, with a salty but less fishy taste, this clear, deep pink sauce is made along the Italian Amalfi coast from salted anchovies. It is the modern equivalent of *garum*, a sauce popular in Ancient Rome made from fermented whole fish, including the guts and blood, which was used instead of salt to season food.

Oyster sauce

A thick sauce made from ground oysters, water, salt, cornflour and caramel, oyster sauce is added to stir-fries and is a popular condiment in Chinese cooking. It is worth looking for brands that do not include MSG. Refrigerate after opening to prevent it developing mould.

Shrimp paste

Also known as *kapi*, *trassi*, *trassie*, *terasi*, *ngapi*, *blacan*, *belacan* and *xiajiang*, this dense mixture of fermented ground shrimp is used extensively in Southeast Asian cuisines and is sold in blocks or ground. Many different types are made, ranging from *ngapi yay*, a watery condiment popular in Burmese cuisine, to pink pastes that are added to curries, and darker ones, like the thick, syrupy Hokkien *hae ko* or *petis udang* from Malaysia, that are used for dipping sauces. In the Philippines, the dark, sweet *bagoong alamang* is used as a topping for green mango. Shrimp paste should be cooked before eating.

Fish balls

Made from ground fish, these are a popular street food in South China, especially Hong Kong where two kinds of fish balls are sold. The first, made from cheaper fish, are small, yellow and sometimes flavoured with spices, with five to seven balls typically being threaded onto bamboo skewers at street stalls. The second kind are bigger, white and made from prime fish and are usually eaten with noodles or added to soups and Mongolian fire pots.

Fish balls are also popular in Thailand, Malaysia and Singapore where they are grilled or fried as street food. They are also added to soups and in Singapore one type, known as *fuzhon*, is stuffed with pork.

In the Philippines, fish balls made from cuttlefish or pollock tend to be flatter and are served with a sweet–sour or sweet–spicy dipping sauce.

Gefilte fish are poached fish patties or balls made from ground fish, usually carp or pike, and are eaten by the Ashkenazi Jewish community.

Prawn roe noodles

In China, prawn roe is generally used as a seasoning for tofu or mild-flavoured vegetable dishes but it is also added to wheatflour noodles. Usually sold dried, the noodles can be flavoured with either fresh prawns or their roe and are cut into fine strips like vermicelli, then either left straight or coiled into

small nests. Delicate and with no fishy taste, they are quite grey in colour and, being precooked before drying, only need soaking in boiling water for a few minutes before serving. Their subtle flavour makes them a delicacy in China.

Surimi
(alternative name kani)

yu jiang (Chinese)

This method of processing white fish, so that its flavour and texture mimic that of shellfish, was developed over 900 years ago in Asia. The fish, usually *iytori* (threadfin bream) in Japan and pollock or hake elsewhere, is rinsed, seasoned, minced to a paste and cooked, before being flavoured and cut into sticks and other shapes. Eaten as a cheaper alternative to lobster, crab or king prawns in the West, where products can be known as seafood sticks, sea legs or prawn-flavoured tails, in the East surimi is enjoyed in its own right. In Japan, *kamaboko* fishcakes and fish sausages are made from surimi.

RECIPES

Every country has its signature ways of cooking fish, but the more you explore the world's cuisines, the more you find similar dishes served in different ways, whether it's a robust stew, thin slices of cured fish arranged on a platter or just a fried fillet of cod. For centuries, travellers nostalgic for a taste of home adapted their own recipes to use local ingredients and gradually these hybrid dishes became part of their adopted country's cuisine.

The following recipes are just a taste of the many fish dishes enjoyed in the four corners of the world. Easy to prepare and simple enough to be tackled by a kitchen novice, they will hopefully persuade you to try something new next time you have fish-loving family or friends around your dining table.

Sesame prawn toasts

Serve these warm as party nibbles, piled on a platter with a bowl of Asian dipping sauce such as plum or sweet-and-sour alongside, and watch them disappear!

Makes 24

14 oz raw medium-sized
prawns, peeled and
coarsely chopped
1 slice of ham, chopped
4 spring onions, chopped
1 egg white, lightly beaten
1 tsp finely grated fresh ginger
2 tsp light soy sauce
1 tsp sugar
1 tsp sesame oil or a few drops
of toasted sesame oil
6 large thin slices of white
bread, crusts removed
3 tbsp sesame seeds
oil, for deep-frying

Put the prawns, ham and spring onions in a food processor and blend to a paste. Scrape into a bowl and stir in the egg white, ginger, soy sauce, sugar and sesame oil.

Cut each slice of bread into four squares and spread the shrimp paste over them quite thickly. Sprinkle with the sesame seeds.

Heat oil for deep-frying to 180°C (350°F) and deep-fry the bread squares, three or four at a time, paste-side down, for 2 minutes. Flip them over and fry for 2 minutes more or until golden brown and crisp.

Remove with a slotted spoon and drain on paper towels. Serve warm with a dipping sauce.

Variations: Try adding finely chopped shallots, coriander or a deseeded fresh chilli to the shrimp paste instead of the spring onions.

Seared tuna with shredded vegetables

Adjust the cooking time for the tuna depending on the thickness of the steaks and how rare you like your fish.

Serves 4

280g (10oz) daikon
(white radish)
2 carrots
1 courgette
2 tbsp vegetable oil
Four 150g (5oz) tuna steaks
finely grated zest and juice
of 2 limes
1 tsp finely grated
fresh ginger
2 tbsp mirin or 2 tsp
brown sugar
4 tbsp dark soy sauce
1 tsp sesame seeds
2 tbsp finely chopped mint

Peel the daikon and carrots and trim the courgette. Cut the vegetables into long thin strips and blanch in a pan of boiling water for 2 minutes or until starting to soften. Drain and keep warm in a low oven.

Heat the oil in a heavy frying pan and when very hot add the tuna steaks and cook for 1 to 2 minutes on each side.

Mix together the lime zest and juice, ginger, mirin or sugar and soy sauce, stirring until the sugar dissolves (if using). Pour over the tuna and let bubble for 1 minute.

Toss the vegetables with the sesame seeds and half the mint. Divide between serving plates and top with the tuna steaks, spooning over the juices from the pan. Serve sprinkled with the remaining mint.

Variations: Other oily fish fillets such as mackerel, tuna, marlin, swordfish or salmon can be used.

Sole meunière with tartar sauce

A classic French way of serving a classic fish; the richness of the buttery cooking juices is balanced by the sharpness of the tartar sauce.

Serves 4

To make the tartar sauce, stir all the sauce ingredients together. Season the flour with salt and pepper, to taste.

To cook the fish, dust the sole fillets with the seasoned flour. Heat the olive oil in a large frying pan and fry the fillets for 2 minutes on each side until golden.

Remove the fish from the pan, add the butter, and when it melts and foams, pour in the lemon juice. Return the fish to the pan and baste with the buttery juices.

Serve with the pan juices spooned over, accompanied with the tartar sauce and new potatoes.

Variations: Dover sole is traditionally cooked on the bone à la meunière and then filleted before serving, but due to the high price they now command fillets from other flat fish such as lemon sole or flounder have become a more economical choice.

4 150g (5oz sole) fillets
flour
salt and pepper
3 tbsp light olive oil
6 tbsp butter
juice of 1 lemon

For the sauce:

6 tbsp mayonnaise
1 tbsp finely chopped gherkin
2 tsp chopped capers
1 tbsp chopped parsley
1 small shallot, finely chopped

Devilled whitebait with gremolata

Gremolata is a tangy mix of parsley, garlic and lemon zest that Italians sprinkle over strongly flavoured dishes to give them a fresh, citrus lift. Commonly used with rich meat stews like osso buco, it also works well with fried fish.

Serves 4

100g (4oz) all-purpose flour
½ tsp hot chilli powder
salt and pepper
700g (1lb 9oz) whitebait
oil, for deep-frying
lemon wedges

For the gremolata:
finely grated zest of 1 lemon
3 tbsp finely chopped
flat-leaf parsley
2 garlic cloves, finely chopped

To make the gremolata, mix the lemon zest, parsley and garlic together.

To cook the whitebait, put the flour, chilli powder and salt and freshly ground black pepper to taste in a large plastic food bag. Rinse the whitebait in a colander, pat dry with paper towels and add to the bag. Shake well so the whitebait are coated with the flour.

Heat oil for deep-frying to 190°C (375°F) and deep-fry the whitebait in three or four batches for about 3 minutes each batch, until the fish are lightly golden and crisp.

Drain on paper towels and serve at once sprinkled with the gremolata and with lemon wedges to squeeze over.

Variations: Instead of gremolata, the whitebait can be served with tartar sauce or mayonnaise spiked with a little fresh chilli.

Seafood laksa

A speciality of the Malay peninsula where coconut milk is used as the base for many sauces and soups. In the local food markets customers are more likely to drop in for a bowl of *laksa* as a midmorning pick-me-up rather than eating it as a lunch or supper dish.

Serves 4

Put the coconut milk, lemongrass, fish sauce, ginger, mushrooms, lime juice, sugar and mangetout in a large pan and simmer gently for 10 minutes. Avoid letting the mixture boil hard or the coconut milk will separate.

When the coconut broth is almost ready, heat the oil in a wok or large frying pan and stir-fry the seafood for 2 to 3 minutes until the prawns turn pink and the squid, white fish and scallops are opaque.

Divide the seafood between serving bowls and spoon the broth over. Garnish with the chopped coriander.

Variations: Already special, this fish stew can be made even more indulgent with the addition of crayfish or lobster tails.

350ml (12 fl oz)
coconut milk
2 lemongrass stalks, cut
into 5cm (2in) lengths
1 tbsp fish sauce
1 tsp finely grated fresh ginger
100g (4oz) sliced mushrooms
juice of 1 lime
1 tsp sugar
50g (2oz) mangetout, halved
lengthways
2 tbsp oil
8 raw jumbo prawns, halved
lengthways and deveined
150g (6oz) squid, cleaned and
cut into bite-size pieces
150g (6oz) firm white fish
fillet, eg monkfish, cut into
bite-sized pieces
8 scallops
2 tbsp chopped coriander

Crisp curled squid with sweet chilli sauce

If using squid that has previously been frozen, thaw it completely and blot dry with paper towels before frying because any residual moisture could cause the hot oil to spit.

Serves 4

500g (1lb 2oz) squid, cleaned
and cut into small pieces
3 tbsp cornflour
salt and pepper
oil, for deep-frying

For the sauce:
100g (4oz) large red chillies,
deseeded and chopped
3 garlic cloves, crushed
150ml (5 fl oz) rice vinegar
150g (5oz) brown sugar
2 tbsp light soy sauce
1 green chilli, deseeded
and chopped

To make the chilli sauce, put the red chillies, garlic, rice vinegar and sugar in a pan and heat gently until the sugar dissolves. Simmer until the liquid reduces to a syrup, then stir in the soy sauce and green chilli and leave to cool.

To cook the squid, lightly score the pieces in a criss-cross pattern with a sharp knife, taking care not to cut right through the flesh. Season the cornflour with a little salt and plenty of black pepper and use to dust the squid until evenly coated.

Heat oil for deep-frying to 180°C (350°F) and fry the squid in two or three batches for about 2 minutes each batch, or until golden and crisp. Drain on paper towels and serve hot with the chilli sauce.

Variations: Instead of squid, cut fillets from flat fish such as sole or flounder into strips, coat in seasoned flour or herbed breadcrumbs, deep-fry and serve with the chilli sauce.

Ceviche tuna in a citrus dressing

To make the fish easier to slice, wrap it tightly in plastic wrap and chill it in the refrigerator for about 1 hour so it is firm but not solid. Use a non-serrated carving knife, or similar knife with a long, thin blade for slicing, and cut through the tuna using a sawing motion.

Serves 4

Slice the tuna as thinly as possible and arrange on a serving platter. Sprinkle with the shallots and basil leaves.

To make the dressing, mix together the soy sauce, orange juice, lime juice and sugar, stirring until the sugar dissolves. Spoon over the tuna.

Let stand for 10 to 15 minutes before serving, and garnish with the orange rind.

Variations: Salmon or fillets from a firm white fish could be used instead of tuna – it is important that the fish is as fresh as possible.

400g (14oz) fresh sushi-grade tuna
2 shallots, finely chopped
4 basil leaves, very finely sliced

For the dressing:
3 tbsp light soy sauce
2 tbsp fresh orange juice
1 tbsp lime juice
1 tbsp caster sugar
fine shreds of orange rind, to garnish.

Oysters Rockefeller

Created at Antoine's Restaurant in New Orleans in 1899 when chef Jules Alciatore was looking for a way of serving the local gulf oysters, which were in plentiful supply. Legend has it that on trying the dish, a customer exclaimed, "Why, this is as rich as Rockefeller!"

Serves 4

Line a grill pan or roasting pan with crumpled foil so the oysters can sit upright in it without spilling their juices.

Heat a quarter of the butter in a frying pan, add the shallots and celery and cook gently until softened. Add the parsley and spinach and continue to cook until the spinach has wilted.

Transfer the mixture to a food processor. Cut up the remaining butter into small pieces and add with the breadcrumbs, Tabasco and Pernod. Blend until smooth.

Preheat the grill.

Put 1 tbsp of the mixture on top of each oyster and grill for 3 to 4 minutes until the butter melts and the tops are crisp and golden. Serve warm – plenty of chilled champagne is the traditional accompaniment!

Variations: Mussels or scallops could be topped with the spinach mixture and grilled or oven-baked.

24 rock oysters, opened
225g (8oz) butter
4 shallots, chopped
1 celery stalk, chopped
4 tbsp chopped parsley
200g (7oz) spinach leaves,
coarse stalks removed and
leaves shredded
85g (3oz) fresh
breadcrumbs
A dash of Tabasco sauce
2 tbsp Pernod or another
aniseed liqueur

Red mullet Provençal

Powerful Mediterranean flavours like olives, anchovies, capers and tomatoes work well with a richly flavoured oily fish like red mullet. Crusty bread and fine green beans make good accompaniments.

Serves 4

Heat half the olive oil in a pan, add the shallots and garlic and fry until both are soft and golden. Add the capers, olives, anchovies, tomatoes and wine and simmer for about 10 minutes until the liquid reduces and the sauce is quite thick.

Preheat the grill.

Line the grill pan with foil and lay the fish on it. Brush the mullet with the remaining olive oil and season with plenty of freshly ground black pepper. Grill for about 5 minutes on each side until cooked.

Stir the lemon juice and parsley into the sauce and serve with the fish.

Variations: The Provençal sauce works well with other full-flavoured fish such as mackerel, salmon or tuna.

6 tbsp olive oil
2 shallots, chopped
2 garlic cloves, chopped
1 tbsp capers, rinsed
85g (3oz) pitted black olives,
chopped
30g (1oz) anchovy fillets,
roughly chopped
225g (8oz) tin chopped
tomatoes
1l (4 fl oz) red wine
4 red mullet, cleaned
and scaled
juice of ½ a lemon
2 tbsp chopped parsley

Chargrilled sardines with fresh herbs

Sardines sprinkled with coarse sea salt and grilled over charcoal are most holidaymakers' idea of the perfect lunch after a relaxing morning on the beach. Fresh herb sprigs sprinkled over the fish add their own aromatic flavours.

Serves 4

Light the barbecue or preheat a grill to medium. Rinse the sardines inside and out and pat dry with paper towels.

Cut several slits in the sides of each fish with a sharp knife. Brush half the oil over the sardines, sprinkle with sea salt and tuck herb sprigs in between and inside the fish. Arrange in a single layer on the barbecue or grill or use a special barbecue fish rack.

Cook for 2 to 3 minutes, turn over and brush with the remaining oil. Cook for 2 to 3 minutes more and serve at once with lemon wedges to squeeze over and crusty bread.

Variations: Mackerel, sprats and herring are all excellent chargrilled. As oily fish have thin, papery skin, brushing the fish with oil before grilling helps prevent it burning and peeling away.

12 fresh sardines, cleaned
and scaled
3 tbsp olive oil
coarse sea salt
fresh herb sprigs, eg rosemary,
thyme, fennel, sage

To serve:
lemon wedges
crusty bread

Sizzling king prawns with garlic

A popular tapa in Spain, these succulent prawns need to be cooked over a high heat to retain all their moisture and flavour. Serve with chunks of crusty bread to mop up the garlicky juices.

Serves 4

6 tbsp olive oil

*4 large garlic cloves, peeled
and left whole
12–16 raw king prawns,
unpeeled with heads and
tails left on
2 tbsp chopped marjoram
or parsley*

Heat the oil in a heavy frying pan and fry the garlic cloves over a medium heat until they turn golden – it is important not to burn the garlic because it will taint rather than flavour the oil. Drain the cloves from the pan and discard.

Turn up the heat to high, add the prawns and fry briskly for 2 to 3 minutes until they turn pink.

Sprinkle with the marjoram or parsley, toss together and immediately transfer the prawns to serving plates, pouring over any oil left in the pan. Serve at once with crusty bread.

Variations: Any size of raw prawns can be used, either peeled or unpeeled, but whatever the size only fry the prawns until they turn pink or they will become tough and tasteless.

Nonya monkfish and prawn curry

The Nonya people of Malaysia and Singapore are the descendants of the Chinese merchants who came to trade with the local people and ended up settling in the peninsula's coastal areas. This creamy curry, spiked with fiery chilli and shrimp pastes, is typical of their distinctive cuisine.

Serves 4

Put the coriander seeds, coriander, turmeric, shrimp paste, garlic, ginger, chilli paste and lime juice in a food processor or blender and grind to a thick paste.

Heat the oil in a large frying pan, add the shallots and cook over a gentle heat until softened. Stir in the spice paste and cook gently for an additional 5 minutes, stirring frequently.

Add the prawns and monkfish and stir until coated in the spice mixture. Add the mango, soy sauce and coconut milk and simmer for about 5 minutes until the fish and prawns are opaque.

Serve with lime wedges to squeeze over and boiled rice.

Variations: Monkfish works particularly well in this dish because the firm flesh doesn't break up. Another white fish could be substituted, although avoid those with very moist flesh as too much liquid will seep out and dilute the sauce.

2 tbsp coriander seeds,
lightly crushed
2 tbsp roughly chopped
coriander
2 tsp ground turmeric
½ tsp shrimp paste
2 large garlic cloves, chopped
2.5cm (1in) piece fresh ginger,
peeled and chopped
1 tsp hot chilli paste
juice of 1 lime
2 tbsp oil
3 shallots, sliced
12 raw king prawns, peeled
500g (1lb 2oz) monkfish
fillet, cubed
1 mango, peeled, pitted
and chopped
3 tbsp dark soy sauce
400ml (14 fl oz)
coconut milk

To serve:
lime wedges

Mussels with white wine and sour cream

Most mussels bought from a supermarket or fish merchant will have been cleaned and be ready to cook but, if not, scrub them under cold running water and scrape away any barnacles or "beard".

Serves 4

4 shallots, chopped
2 garlic cloves, chopped
6 tbsp chopped parsley
250ml (8 fl oz) dry white wine
2kg (4½lb) mussels in
their shells
2 tbsp sour cream

Put the shallots, garlic, 2 tbsp of the parsley, the wine and 150ml (5 fl oz) water in a large pan. Bring to the boil, lower the heat and leave to bubble gently for 5 minutes.

Increase the heat so the liquid comes to a vigorous boil, add the mussels and cover the pan with a lid. Cook for about 5 minutes, shaking the pan regularly, until all the mussel shells have opened – discard any that stay tightly closed.

Lift out the mussels with a slotted spoon and pile them into four warm serving bowls. Boil the liquid in the pan for 2 minutes, then beat in the sour cream and season with freshly ground black pepper. Pour over the mussels and sprinkle with the rest of the parsley.

Variations: Clams could be cooked in the same way.

Blackened cod with avocado, pineapple and bean salsa

Blackening is not a ruse to pass off burnt offerings as haute cuisine but refers to the aromatic mix of herbs, garlic and spices that cooks in America's Deep South spread over fish before frying or grilling. A fruity salsa with a chilli kick makes a good accompaniment.

Serves 4

Mix all the salsa ingredients together and spoon into a bowl. If making several hours ahead, add the avocado just before serving to prevent it turning brown.

For the fish, mix together the dried herbs, smoked paprika, ginger, garlic, crushed coriander seeds, half the lime juice and the black pepper until evenly combined. Spread this over the cod fillets and set aside for 15 minutes.

Heat the oil in a heavy frying pan and fry the cod fillets for 5 minutes on each side or until cooked. Remove them from the pan and add the butter and remaining lime juice. Heat until the butter melts and foams and spoon over the fish.

Serve with the salsa.

Variations: Any thick fillets of white fish can be "blackened", as can oily fish like salmon and mackerel.

2 tbsp mixed dried herbs
2 tsp smoked paprika
1 tsp finely grated
fresh ginger
1 garlic clove, crushed
2 tsp crushed coriander seeds
4 tbsp lime juice
½ tsp freshly ground
black pepper
four 175g (6oz) cod fillets
2 tbsp sunflower oil
50g (2oz) butter

For the salsa:

400g (14oz) can red kidney
beans, drained and rinsed
12 cherry tomatoes, halved
2 pineapple rings, chopped
1 avocado, pitted, peeled
and chopped
1 green chilli pepper, deseeded
and finely sliced
2 tbsp white wine vinegar or
lime juice

Lobster gratin with red pepper and mushrooms

The freshest, best-tasting lobster will always be the one you buy live and cook at home but, if you prefer, you can buy ready-cooked ones from your fish merchant for this dish. Add a crisp leafy salad and you have a feast fit for a king.

Serves 4

4 small or 2 large lobsters,
*cooked, split in half
lengthways and cleaned*
1 tbsp olive oil
6 spring onions, finely sliced
*1 red pepper, deseeded and
finely chopped*
*4 portobello mushrooms,
finely chopped*
100ml (4 fl oz) dry white wine
*6 tbsp garlic and herb
cream cheese*
2 tbsp sour cream
*100g (4oz) Gruyère cheese,
grated*

To serve:
lemon wedges

Scoop the meat from the body shell of the lobsters, crack the claws and remove the meat from those as well. Cut the meat into small pieces.

Heat the oil in a frying pan, add the spring onions, pepper and mushrooms, and fry for 5 minutes. Add the wine to the pan and leave to bubble for a couple of minutes. Remove from the heat and leave to cool.

Stir the lobster meat into the vegetables and spoon back into the half-shells, packing the mix in fairly firmly. Preheat the grill to high.

Mash the garlic and herb cream cheese with the sour cream and Gruyère and spread over the lobster filling. Grill for 4 to 5 minutes until the topping turns golden. Serve with lemon wedges to squeeze over.

Variations: Any type of lobster can be used for the dish. If using a spiny or rock lobster, reserve the legs for garnish.

Warm scallop salad with salsa verde

Tiny bay scallops are beautifully sweet and juicy and seared in a hot pan they make an easy and delicious starter or light lunch dish. If you make the salsa verde in advance and it separates, beat it again just before serving.

Serves 4

To make the salsa verde, mix the coriander, basil, parsley, garlic and mustard together. Gradually beat in the olive oil and lemon juice until evenly blended.

To make the salad, heat the oil in a heavy frying pan, add the scallops and sear for 1 minute on each side. Pour over the lemon juice and when the sizzling dies down remove from the heat.

Arrange a mix of lettuce leaves on each serving plate and add the cherry tomato halves. Spoon the scallops on top and drizzle over the salsa verde. Serve at once.

Variations: Larger scallops can replace the bay scallops but reduce the quantity to three per person and increase the cooking time to about 2 minutes per side. Prawns or baby squid could also be cooked and served in the same way.

2 tbsp extra-virgin olive oil
350g (12oz) bay scallops
juice of 1 lemon
mixed lettuce leaves
8 cherry tomatoes, halved

For the salsa verde:
3 tbsp chopped coriander
1 tbsp chopped basil
3 tbsp chopped parsley
2 garlic cloves, finely chopped
1 tbsp Dijon mustard
100ml (4 fl oz) extra-virgin olive oil
juice of 1 lemon

Smoked salmon with blinis and caviar

Blinis are small yeast pancakes that are traditionally eaten in Russia topped with sour cream, smoked fish and caviar.

Serves 4

To make the blinis, put the flour in a food processor and mix in the yeast. Beat the egg yolk with the sugar and add to the dry ingredients with the salt and warm water, blending until evenly mixed. Cover with a damp cloth and leave in a warm place until the yeast mixture has doubled in size.

Mix in the milk to make a thick batter, transfer it to a bowl, cover and leave until small bubbles appear on the surface. Beat the egg white until standing in stiff peaks and fold into the batter.

Heat a heavy frying pan, add a small piece of butter, and swirl until it coats the pan. Spoon in a little of the batter and spread into a 7.5cm (3in) round. Cook until bubbles appear on the surface and the blini has set, then flip it over with a spatula and cook the other side. Keep warm in a low oven while you cook seven more blinis.

4 oz smoked salmon slices
4 tbsp sour cream
2 tbsp caviar

Serve the blinis warm, topped with smoked salmon, sour cream and caviar.

For the blinis:
140g (5oz) wholewheat flour
1 tsp instant yeast
1 egg, separated
a pinch of sugar
a pinch of salt
7 tbsp warm water
7 tbsp warm milk
butter, for frying

Variations: Slices of smoked trout or halibut can top the blinis instead of salmon, or try bite-sized chunks of smoked mackerel or eel. Substitute lumpfish or salmon roe if your budget doesn't stretch to caviar!

Thai-style marinated mackerel

Light and aromatic, this fresh-tasting starter is equally delicious served warm or cold.

Serves 4

Toast the coriander seeds in a dry heavy frying pan until they smell aromatic, remove, and add to the olive oil.

Put 4 tbsp water, the fish sauce, rice vinegar, sugar, lemongrass and ginger in a pan and slowly bring to the boil, stirring until the sugar dissolves. Add the mackerel fillets, flesh-side down, and simmer for 3 to 4 minutes or until the fish is just cooked.

1 tbsp coriander seeds
4 tbsp extra-virgin olive oil
1 tbsp Thai fish sauce
1 tbsp rice vinegar
4 tsp sugar
1 lemongrass stalk,
sliced lengthways
½ tsp finely grated fresh
ginger
2 mackerel, filleted

Carefully lift from the pan and arrange on serving plates. Add 1 tablespoon of the cooking juices to the oil and coriander seeds and beat to combine. Spoon over the fish and serve warm or cold.

Variations: Other oily fish work well in this dish. Try fillets of salmon or small tuna steaks, searing the fish in hot oil to cook it before pouring over the warm marinade.

Salade Niçoise with beans

A satisfying main meal salad that's packed with good things. The lemon and mustard vinaigrette dressing cuts through the rich flavour of the tuna perfectly.

Serves 4

2 tbsp extra-virgin olive oil
500g (1lb 2oz) fresh
tuna steaks
200g (7oz) green beans,
trimmed
400g (14oz) tin cannellini
beans, drained and rinsed
1 red onion, peeled and
thinly sliced
4 hard-boiled eggs

For the dressing:
5 tbsp extra-virgin olive oil
1 tbsp lemon juice
1 tsp Dijon mustard
1 garlic clove, finely chopped
2 tbsp chopped parsley
a pinch of sugar
salt and pepper

To make the dressing, beat all the ingredients together.

Preheat the grill.

To prepare the salad, brush the olive oil over the tuna and grill for 3 to 4 minutes on each side so the steaks are still slightly pink in the centre. Break up the fish into chunks.

Blanch the green beans in a pan of boiling water for 2 to 3 minutes until just tender. Drain, cool by running cold water through the strainer and pat dry with paper towels.

Put the green beans, cannellini beans, sliced onion and tuna in a serving dish, add half the dressing, and toss lightly together. Cut the hard-boiled eggs into quarters and arrange over the salad. Drizzle over the rest of the dressing and serve with warm crusty bread.

Variations: The salad can be made with tinned tuna rather than fresh to save time. Look for tuna steaks that have been canned in water or oil, and drain well before breaking the fish into large flakes and adding to the other ingredients.

Zarzuela de pescado

Zarzuela actually translates as "operetta", and how this famous Spanish seafood stew got its name is a mystery. To ensure the fish cooks evenly, it is best to use a large pan that is wide and quite shallow. If the pan is deep and narrow, the fish at the bottom of the pot could over-cook.

Serves 4

Heat the oil in a large sauté pan, add the onion and garlic and cook gently until soft but not browned.

Stir in the paprika, cook for 1 minute and then add the tomatoes, oregano, saffron with its soaking water, wine and stock. Simmer gently for 10 minutes.

Add the hake, simmer for 3 minutes, then stir in the seafood, taking care not to break up the pieces of hake. Cook for 2 minutes until the seafood is piping hot, season to taste, and sprinkle in the parsley.

Serve at once with toasted bread croûtons.

Variations: Hake is a highly prized fish in Spain, but another firm white fish such as monkfish or a selection of different fish could be substituted according to what is available.

2 tbsp olive oil
1 onion, finely chopped
3 garlic cloves, chopped
2 tsp paprika
4 tomatoes, peeled, deeeded and chopped
2 tsp chopped fresh oregano or 1 tsp dried oregano
a pinch of saffron threads, soaked in a little warm water for 5 minutes
150ml (5 fl oz) dry white wine
225ml (8 fl oz) fish stock
1kg (2lb) hake fillets, skinned and cut into chunks
350g (12oz) mixed prepared seafood (mussels, prawns, squid), defrosted if frozen
salt and pepper
2 tbsp chopped parsley

To serve:
bread croûtons

Escabeche de sardinas

A tangy marinade of spices, herbs and vinegar is widely used in Spain to preserve fish. Although white fish fillets can be prepared *en escabeche*, the dish is most successful made with oily fish because the vinegar provides a good contrast to their rich flavour.

Serves 4

*16 sardines, scaled, cleaned
and heads removed
4 tbsp flour
4 tbsp olive oil
1 onion, sliced into rings
2 garlic cloves, finely chopped
1 tsp paprika
1 dried red chilli,
finely chopped, or 1 tsp dried
red chilli flakes
3 bay leaves
3 thyme sprigs
2 whole cloves
100ml (4 fl oz) sherry vinegar
100ml (4 fl oz) dry white wine
salt and pepper*

Rinse the sardines to remove any loose scales, pat dry with paper towels and dust with the flour. Heat half the olive oil in a frying pan and fry the sardines for 2 to 3 minutes on each side. Drain from the pan and lay them side by side in a large, shallow, non-metallic dish.

Wipe out the pan with paper towels and add the rest of the oil. Fry the onion and garlic gently until softened, add the paprika and dried chilli and fry for 1 minute. Add the bay leaves, thyme and cloves and cook for 1 minute more.

Pour in the vinegar and wine and season with a little salt and freshly ground black pepper. Bring to a simmer, remove the pan from the heat and let the liquid cool for 10 minutes before pouring over the sardines.

When completely cold, cover and chill in the refrigerator for 24 hours before bringing back to room temperature to serve.

Variations: Other oily fish such as mackerel, herring or sprats could also be used.

Chickpea and herb-crusted cod

The crunchy topping for the fish is given an Asian twist with the addition of ginger and a splash of soy sauce, while crushed chickpeas replace the more usual breadcrumbs.

Serves 4

50g (2oz) dried chickpeas,
soaked overnight
2 tbsp olive oil
four 175g (6oz) cod fillets
juice of 1 lemon
1 tbsp finely grated
fresh ginger
ground black pepper
1 tbsp snipped chives
2 tbsp chopped parsley
1 tbsp light soy sauce

To serve:
lemon wedges

Drain the chickpeas and rub off the skins. Heat the olive oil in a pan, add the chickpeas and fry until they turn a cream colour. Drain on paper towels and leave to cool before grinding to fine crumbs in a food processor.

Preheat the oven to 200°C (400°F).

Place the cod fillets side by side in a greased ovenproof dish and squeeze over the lemon juice. Spread the ginger over the fillets and season with freshly ground black pepper. Cover the dish with foil and bake for 10 minutes.

Mix together the chickpea crumbs, chives, parsley and soy sauce. Remove the fish from the oven, discard the foil and spread the chickpea mixture over each fillet, pressing it down lightly with the back of a spoon.

Return the dish uncovered to the oven and bake for 10 minutes. Serve with lemon wedges to squeeze over and a green vegetable.

Variations: The crusty topping works well with other fish such as halibut, salmon or bream fillets.

Penne with salmon in a creamy saffron sauce

A luxurious pasta dish that's colourful, quick, and easy to prepare. It works equally well as a family lunch dish or as a special supper for friends.

Serves 4

150ml (5 fl oz) hot vegetable or fish stock
a pinch of saffron threads
50g (2oz) butter
6 spring onions, trimmed and chopped
1 garlic clove, crushed
5 tbsp dry white wine
150ml (5 fl oz) double cream
225g (8oz) frozen peas
400g (14oz) penne pasta
350g (12oz) salmon fillet, skinned and cut into pieces

Pour the hot stock into a small bowl and crumble in the saffron threads. Infuse for 5 minutes.

Melt the butter in a large pan, add the spring onions and garlic and cook gently for 1 minute. Add the wine, let bubble for 1 minute and then add the stock and saffron threads, cream and peas. Let the mixture simmer gently while you cook the pasta.

Bring a large pan of water to the boil, add the penne and boil for 8 minutes or until it is al dente. When the pasta is almost ready, stir the salmon into the cream sauce and cook gently for 2 to 3 minutes.

Drain the penne and stir into the salmon mixture. Serve at once.

Variations: Instead of salmon, peeled raw prawns or a mixture of prawns and mussels could be added to the sauce.

Ocean pie

If you're looking for comfort food, a hearty fish pie takes a lot of beating. This recipe mixes white fish and smoked fish with juicy prawns and is topped with a crisp potato thatch.

Serves 4

Peel the potatoes and cut into even-sized chunks. Boil them in a pan of water until tender, then drain and mash with the butter. Stir in the capers and add seasoning to taste.

Preheat the grill.

Cut the cod and smoked haddock into bite-sized pieces and grill for 5 minutes until cooked. Carefully transfer to an ovenproof dish without breaking up the pieces and add the prawns and egg quarters. Spoon the cheese sauce over the fish, prawns and eggs in an even layer.

Preheat the oven to 200°C (400°F). Heap the mashed potatoes over the fish mixture, pressing down evenly with a fork. Lift the pie onto a baking sheet and bake for 30 minutes until the potatoes are golden. Serve with the chives sprinkled over.

Variations: Almost any combination of fish can be used for the pie although, while salmon or trout could be added, avoid very oily fish like sardines or mackerel as they would be too rich with the cheese sauce.

200g (1lb 9oz) potatoes
50g (2oz) butter
2 tbsp unsalted bottled capers, rinsed
Salt and pepper
250g (9oz) cod fillet, skinned
250g (9oz) smoked haddock fillet, skinned
175g (6oz) peeled prawns
2 hard-boiled eggs, quartered
400ml (14 fl oz) four-cheese sauce for pasta, or similar thick cheese sauce
2 tbsp snipped chives

Seafood cocktails with avocado dressing

A variation on the traditional seafood cocktail, this recipe dresses the crab and prawns with an avocado sauce rather than the familiar pink marie rose sauce. If you're a stickler for the traditional, omit the avocado and simply stir a couple of tablespoons of tomato ketchup into the other dressing ingredients.

Serves 4

Arrange a little shredded lettuce in the base of each serving dish and top with the orange segments, chopped avocado, prawn and crab meat, dividing the ingredients equally between the dishes.

To make the dressing, put the avocado, mayonnaise, sour cream and lime juice in a blender and process until smooth. If the dressing is too thick, thin it down by stirring in a little warm water.

Spoon the dressing over each salad and sprinkle with the parsley.

shredded lettuce
2 oranges, peeled
and segmented
1 avocado, pitted, peeled
and chopped
350g (12oz) peeled prawns
200g (7oz) white crab meat,
flaked
4 tbsp chopped parsley

For the dressing:
1 avocado, pitted, peeled
and chopped
6 tbsp mayonnaise
4 tbsp low-fat sour cream
juice of 2 limes

Variations: Other seafood such as clams, mussels, chopped lobster or crayfish meat can be used to make the cocktails.

Fish tikka masala

A creamy curry from India that is a mouth-watering mix of vegetables and white fish, the spicy sauce being cooled and enriched by the addition of plain yogurt. Serve with rice or naan bread, pappadams and mango chutney.

Serves 4

Cook the carrots and halved potatoes in a pan of boiling water for 5 minutes until almost tender. Drain.

Heat the oil in a large pan and fry the onion gently until softened. Add the aubergine, carrots and potatoes and fry for 10 minutes, stirring occasionally. Stir in the curry paste until the vegetables are coated, pour in the stock and add the tomato purée.

Mix the cornflour and yogurt together until smooth and add to the pan. Bring to the boil, stirring constantly until the sauce has thickened, then lower the heat, cover and simmer for 20 minutes.

Add the fish and cook for 5 minutes until the chunks turn opaque. Sprinkle with the coriander and serve at once.

Variations: Instead of white fish, the curry could be made with raw prawns or a mixture of fish and prawns.

2 carrots, sliced
175g (6oz) new potatoes
2 tbsp oil
1 onion, thinly sliced
1 aubergine, trimmed and cut into small chunks
2 tbsp tikka masala curry paste
400ml (14 fl oz) fish or vegetable stock
2 tbsp tomato purée
2 tsp cornflour
4 tbsp thick plain yogurt
700g (1lb 9oz) firm white fish fillets, eg monkfish, haddock, whiting or orange roughy, skinned and cut into chunks
2 tbsp chopped coriander

Jerk snapper with papaya salsa

Long before Christopher Columbus arrived in the West Indies, native Arawak Indians preserved fish by rubbing it with spices and acidic chillies. These early seasoning rubs have developed into the "jerk" spice mixes of today and they are still popular throughout the Caribbean islands, particularly in Jamaica. If the salsa is made in advance, its flavours will have time to develop.

Serves 4

Preheat the oven to 200°C (400°F).

*1 red pepper, deseeded
and chopped
1 red chilli, deseeded and
chopped
2 garlic cloves, chopped
1 tsp finely grated
fresh ginger
1 tsp ground coriander
4 tbsp white wine vinegar
4 tbsp dark soy sauce
3 tbsp sunflower oil
four 175g (6oz) snapper fillets*

Put the pepper in a food processor with the red chilli, garlic and ginger and blitz until finely chopped. Add the coriander, vinegar, soy sauce and 1 tbsp of the oil and blitz again until smooth.

Slash the skin of the snapper fillets several times with a sharp knife and lay in a single layer in a greased, shallow ovenproof dish. Rub the spice mix over the fish until well covered.

Bake the fish in the oven for 10 minutes or until cooked.

To make the salsa, place the papaya, palm hearts, watermelon, green chilli, coriander and lime juice in a bowl and stir until mixed. Serve the salsa with the fish and accompany with rice and pigeon peas.

For the salsa:
*1 papaya, peeled, deseeded
and chopped
3 tinned palm hearts, chopped
1 small slice of watermelon,
deseeded and chopped
1 green chilli, deseeded and
finely chopped
1 tbsp chopped coriander
juice of 1 lime*

Variations: The jerk mix can be used with any type of fish that has a strong enough flavour to take on the spices, such as red mullet, salmon or mackerel.

Clam, sweet potato and sweetcorn chowder

A variation on the hearty soup made famous by the clam shacks of New England, where clams are prolific and feature in all sorts of recipes from fritters and bakes to salads and stews. Serve it in deep bowls with hunks of French bread.

Serves 6

Cook the sweet potatoes in a pan of boiling water until tender. Drain and mash a quarter of them, leaving the rest in chunks.

Put the clams in another pan, add 4 tbsp water, cover and cook for 5 minutes until the shells open. Drain, and when cool enough to handle, pick the meat out of the shells.

Heat the oil in a large pan, add the leeks and celery, cover and cook over a low heat for 10 minutes until softened. Mix the flour with a few tablespoons of the stock until smooth and stir into the pan with the rest of the stock, the thyme and the mashed sweet potato. Bring to the boil, stirring until thickened and smooth, and simmer for 5 minutes.

Stir in the cream, sweetcorn, sweet potato chunks and clams and season to taste. Simmer for 5 minutes more then serve at once.

500g (1lb 2oz) sweet potatoes, peeled and cut into small chunks
500g (1lb 2oz) clams
2 tbsp sunflower oil
2 leeks, trimmed and thinly sliced
1 celery stalk, chopped
1 tbsp plain flour
600ml (20 fl oz) fish or vegetable stock
1 tsp chopped thyme
175ml (6 fl oz) double cream
100g (4oz) sweetcorn

Variations: Instead of sweet potatoes, chunks of pumpkin, butternut squash or ordinary potatoes can be used. The clams could also be replaced with equal quantities of peeled raw prawns stirred in with the cream and sweetcorn and cooked, smoked haddock or cod, broken into large flakes added just before serving.

Gingered crab cakes

The fresher and sweeter the crab meat you can find, the better flavour these crisp-coated cakes will have. Mini versions of the crab cakes can be served with a spicy tomato dipping sauce as a pre-dinner nibble.

Serves 4

Put the potatoes in a bowl and mix in the spring onions, garlic, ginger, anchovies, lime zest, coriander, parsley and crab meat. Add seasoning to taste.

Shape the mixture into eight balls, place on a plate and chill for 30 minutes to firm them up.

350g (12oz) potatoes, boiled and mashed
4 spring onions, trimmed and chopped
2 garlic cloves, crushed
1 tsp finely grated fresh ginger
30g (1oz) anchovy fillets, chopped
finely grated zest of 1 lime
2 tbsp chopped coriander
2 tbsp chopped parsley
400g (14oz) white crab meat
salt and pepper
100g (4oz) fresh white breadcrumbs
flour, for dusting
2 eggs, beaten
oil, for deep-frying

Spread out the breadcrumbs on a plate. Dust the crab cakes with flour, brush with beaten egg and press in the breadcrumbs until coated.

Heat oil for deep-frying to 182°C (360°F) and fry in two batches for 7 to 8 minutes each or until golden brown and crisp.

Serve at once with mayonnaise and a green salad.

Variations: Half the crab meat could be replaced with finely chopped raw prawns.

Paella Valenciana

Spain's most famous dish originates from Valencia, where fish and seafood are plentiful and the special short-grain *calasparra* rice, used in all true paellas, is produced in the small village of Calasparra in the neighbouring province of Murcia. You can cook the dish in a large, heavy frying pan if you don't have one of the traditional two-handled black paella pans.

Serves 4

Heat the oil in a paella or other frying pan, add the onion and fry over a gentle heat until soft. Add the red and green peppers and fry for 5 minutes, stirring occasionally. Stir the rice and paprika into the pan and cook for 1 minute. Pour in the saffron and its soaking water, the wine and stock and stir well. Simmer for 20 to 25 minutes or until the rice is almost tender, stirring occasionally.

Stir in the peas, prawns and squid and spread the mussels on top. Cook for an additional 10 minutes or until the rice is cooked, the prawns have turned pink and the mussel shells open (discard any that stay tightly closed).

Variations: If your pan isn't big enough to accommodate all the mussels in their shells, cook them in a separate pan and then add them to the cooked paella. Chunks of white fish or bay scallops can be added to the mix of seafood.

2 tbsp olive oil
1 large Spanish onion, sliced
1 red pepper, deseeded
and chopped
1 green pepper, deseeded and
chopped
350g (12oz) calasparra
rice (use risotto rice if not
available)
1 tsp smoked paprika
a pinch of saffron threads,
soaked in 2 tbsp warm water
for 5 minutes
150ml (5 fl oz) dry white wine
400ml (14 fl oz) fish stock
175g (6oz) frozen peas
250g (9oz) raw prawns, peeled
150g (5oz) cleaned squid, cut
into rings
1kg (2¼lb) mussels in their
shells, scrubbed

Pollock with chorizo and cherry tomatoes

An often underrated white fish, pollock is as versatile as cod but far more sustainable. The thick fillets have an excellent flavour that goes well with other strong tastes such as chorizo and fresh herbs.

Serves 4

Cook the peeled potatoes in a pan of boiling water until tender. Drain and chop into small chunks.

Heat 2 tbsp of the olive oil in a large frying pan and cook the onion over a low heat until softened. Add the yellow pepper and chorizo and fry for 5 minutes, stirring occasionally. Remove the mixture from the pan and set aside.

500g (1lb 2oz) potatoes
6 tbsp olive oil
1 onion, sliced
1 yellow pepper, deseeded
and chopped
150g (5oz) chorizo, sliced or
cut into small chunks
2 tsp finely chopped
rosemary leaves
1 tbsp chopped oregano
four 175g (6oz) pollock fillets
8 cherry tomatoes, halved
150ml (5 fl oz) fresh
orange juice
1 tsp honey
2 tbsp tomato purée

Add another tbsp of olive oil to the pan, tip in the potatoes and fry over a medium heat for about 10 minutes until they are golden and crisp, turning the potatoes over regularly.

While the potatoes are cooking, mix the remaining oil with the rosemary and oregano. Preheat the grill. Line a grill pan with greased foil, lay the pollock fillets on it, skin side up, and brush with half the oil and herb mixture.

Grill for 3 minutes, turn the fillets over and brush with the remaining herb oil. Grill for 3 to 4 minutes more, or until the fish is cooked.

Return the onion, pepper and chorizo mix to the frying pan, add the cherry tomatoes and cook for 3 to 4 minutes until everything is heated through and the tomatoes have softened but not collapsed. Divide between four serving plates and place the pollock fillets on top.

Wipe out the frying pan, add the orange juice, honey and tomato purée and stir until combined. Bubble until reduced by half, drizzle over the fish and serve.

Variations: Snapper, cod or bass fillets could be used instead of pollock.

Herring stuffed with sun-dried tomatoes and red onion

Serve this as a light meal accompanied by a crisp leafy salad, adding some new potatoes if you want something more substantial. If you're unsure about filleting the fish (see page 21), ask your fishmonger to do it for you.

Serves 4

Preheat the oven to 200°C (400°F). Fillet the herring according to the instructions on page 21.

Heat the oil in a pan, add the onion and fry gently until softened. Remove from the heat and mix in the breadcrumbs, sun-dried tomatoes, parsley, thyme, lemon zest and juice.

Transfer to a bowl and stir in the beaten eggs until the mixture binds together.

Open out the filleted herrings and place skin side down on a board. Spoon the stuffing mixture down the middle of each fish, fold over and reshape the fish to enclose the stuffing.

Tie up with thin string so the herring keep their shape during cooking and lift them into a greased ovenproof dish.

Bake for 15 minutes or until the herring are cooked. Serve hot with lemon wedges to squeeze over.

Variations: Mackerel, trout or large sardines can be prepared and cooked in the same way.

4 large herring, cleaned and heads removed
2 tbsp olive oil
1 red onion, finely chopped
175g (6oz) fresh breadcrumbs
2 sun-dried tomatoes, finely chopped
2 tbsp chopped parsley
2 tsp thyme leaves
grated zest and juice of 1 lemon, plus extra wedges to squeeze over
2 eggs, beaten

Steamed sea bass with spring onions, coriander and lime

Whole fish make an impressive centrepiece for a dinner party, and steaming them with aromatic Asian herbs and seasonings makes them a healthy dish too.

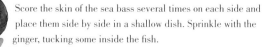

Serves 4

Score the skin of the sea bass several times on each side and place them side by side in a shallow dish. Sprinkle with the ginger, tucking some inside the fish.

Beat together the sesame oil, lime juice, soy sauce and brown sugar, and pour over the fish. Cover and leave in the refrigerator to marinate for 1 hour.

2 1kg (2lb) whole sea bass, scaled and cleaned
2.5cm (1in) piece fresh ginger, peeled and finely chopped
1 tbsp sesame oil
2 tbsp lime juice
4 tbsp soy sauce
2 tsp brown sugar
6 tinned water chestnuts, sliced
1 large carrot, cut into matchsticks
6 spring onions, shredded
200g (7oz) tenderstem broccoli
coriander leaves

Grease a sheet of foil and place the sea bass on it. Lift onto a steaming rack and place over a wok or large pan. Fill the pan one-third with water and put the rack on top. Spoon over any marinade left in the dish and sprinkle the water chestnuts and carrot over and around the fish.

Cover and steam for 15 minutes. Add the spring onions and broccoli and steam for an additional 10 minutes, or until the flesh of the fish flakes easily and the vegetables are tender. Arrange on a serving dish and garnish with coriander leaves. Serve with steamed jasmine rice.

Variations: Other fish such as carp, red snapper, trout,or sea bream can be used. If a fish is too large for your rack, bend it around so it fits inside the steamer. Individual fillets also work well, although the steaming time should be reduced by about half, depending on the thickness of the fish.

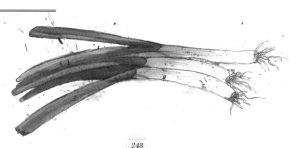

Salmon fishcakes with watercress sauce

The sharp flavour of the watercress sauce makes the ideal accompaniment to these rich-flavoured fishcakes. Baking the potatoes allows most of the moisture to evaporate so the fishcakes are firmer and hold their shape better during cooking.

Serves 4

Preheat the oven to 180°C (350°F).

Wrap the salmon in greased foil and cook in the oven for 25 minutes. Leave to cool before unwrapping and removing the skin and any pin bones. Flake the flesh coarsely into a bowl.

Cut the potato in half, scoop out the flesh and mash. Add to the salmon with the spring onions, parsley and seasoning to taste.

Beat one of the eggs and stir into the mixture to bind it together. Beat the remaining egg in a shallow dish. Shape the fish mixture into four round cakes, dust them with flour, brush with beaten egg and press in the breadcrumbs until evenly coated. Chill for 1 hour or until you are ready to cook.

To make the sauce, blend the watercress, stock and cream in a food processor until smooth and pour into a saucepan. Mix the cornflour with a little water until smooth and stir in. Heat until boiling, stirring constantly, then simmer over a low heat for 5 minutes.

Pan-fry the fishcakes in hot oil until they are golden brown all over. Serve with the watercress sauce.

Variations: Apart from very oily varieties, almost any fish or combination of several different types of fish can be used to make fishcakes. Try mixing equal quantities of white and smoked fish, and using sweet potatoes in place of ordinary ones.

1 large baking potato, about 300g (10½oz) total weight, baked and cooled
500g (1lb 2oz) salmon fillet
3 spring onions, trimmed and finely chopped
2 tbsp chopped parsley
salt and pepper
2 eggs
flour, for dusting
85g (3oz) dry breadcrumbs
oil, for pan-frying

For the sauce:
1 bunch of watercress, tough stalks discarded
150ml (5 fl oz) fish or vegetable stock
125ml (4 fl oz) double cream
1 tsp cornflour

Stamp and go

These Jamaican salt cod fritters got their name from the food stalls that used to sell them wrapped in paper with the word "paid" stamped on the outside – hence "stamp and go". With the advent of refrigeration cod no longer needs to be salted to preserve it, but these little cakes are still popular today.

Serves 4

250g (9oz) salt cod
2 garlic cloves
2 bay leaves
2 tbsp oil, plus extra for deep-frying
1 onion, finely chopped
100g (4oz) plain flour
1 tsp baking powder
1 egg, separated
100ml (4 fl oz) milk
1 tbsp melted butter
2 tbsp chopped coriander
1 tbsp snipped chives
a pinch of cayenne pepper

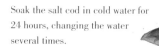

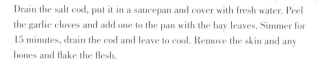

Soak the salt cod in cold water for 24 hours, changing the water several times.

Drain the salt cod, put it in a saucepan and cover with fresh water. Peel the garlic cloves and add one to the pan with the bay leaves. Simmer for 15 minutes, drain the cod and leave to cool. Remove the skin and any bones and flake the flesh.

Crush the second clove of garlic. Heat 2 tbsp oil in a pan and fry the onion and crushed garlic until soft and lightly golden.

Sift the flour and baking powder into a bowl and beat in the egg yolk, milk, melted butter, coriander, chives and cayenne. Add the flaked cod and fried onion and garlic, stirring together until well mixed. Chill in the refrigerator for 1 hour.

Beat the egg white until standing in soft peaks and fold it into the cod mixture.

Heat oil for deep-frying to 180°C (350°F) and, using a large spoon, drop small balls of the mixture into the oil. Fry for 3 to 4 minutes until golden brown and crisp. Drain and serve hot.

Variations: Unsalted cod or another white fish could be used to make the fritters, although they won't have as strong a flavour. The fritters could also be made using chopped raw prawns instead of fish.

Tuna empanadas

"Fast food" Spanish-style, empanadas are popular across Latin America too. In Mexico and South America the crisp pastry parcels would most likely be stuffed with a spicy meat or salsa mixture but in Galicia in northwest Spain, tuna is a popular filling.

Makes about 12

To make the pastry, sift the flour, baking powder and paprika into a mixing bowl. Cut up the butter and vegetable shortening into small pieces, add to the dry ingredients and blend in until the mixture is like fine crumbs. Stir in enough cold water to make a soft dough. Knead until smooth then wrap in plastic wrap and chill for 1 hour.

To make the filling, grill the tuna steaks until just cooked, remove any skin and flake the fish into a bowl.

Heat the oil in a pan and fry the onion and pepper until softened. Remove from the heat and stir in the tomatoes, flaked tuna, parsley and sour cream.

Roll out the pastry thinly and cut into 12.5–15cm (5–6in) rounds, using a pastry cutter or small saucer as a template, gathering up and rerolling the pastry trimmings as necessary.

Preheat the oven to 180°C (350°F).

Spoon the tuna filling onto one half of each pastry round, brush the edges with beaten egg and fold over, pressing the edges together to seal. Lay the empanadas on a baking sheet and brush with beaten egg. Cut a small steam hole in the top of each.

Bake for 15 to 20 minutes or until golden brown. Serve hot or cold.

Variations: Try using other fish in the filling such as salmon or mackerel, and if you like things hot, add a finely chopped chilli to the mix.

500g (1lb 2oz) tuna steaks
2 tbsp olive oil
1 small onion, finely chopped
1 green pepper, deseeded and
finely chopped
2 tomatoes, peeled, deseeded
and finely diced
2 tbsp chopped parsley
4 tbsp sour cream
beaten egg, for brushing

For the pastry:
500g (1lb 2oz)
plain flour
2 tsp baking powder
½ tsp paprika
50g (2oz) butter
50g (2oz) vegetable shortening

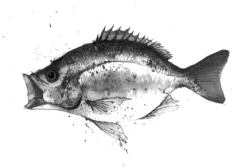

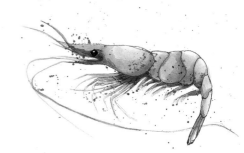

BIBLIOGRAPHY

Alan Davidson, Mediterranean Seafood (Penguin Books, 1972)
Alan Davidson, North Atlantic Seafood (Penguin Books, 1980)
Alan Davidson, Seafood of South-East Asia (Prospect Books, 2003)
Aliza Green, Field Guide to Seafood (Quirk Books, 2007)
Sophie Grigson and William Black, Fish (Headline, 2000)

ACKNOWLEDGMENTS

I would also like to thank the following for their help in writing this book:

Sea Fish Industry Authority, Edinburgh
Monterey Bay Aquarium, California
Tourism Authority of Thailand
Butlers Fishmongers, Westcliff on Sea, Essex
And Asian Pearl, Leleu & Morris, Selsea, Barton & Hart, Fawsitt Fish, all traders at Billingsgate
fish market, London